Scout Speak
Thinking and Talking About Being an NFL Evaluator

Neil Stratton

To my parents, Walt and Paula Stratton.
I can't imagine having a better mom and dad.

TABLE OF CONTENTS

FOREWORD
Jeff Ireland, Assistant GM,
New Orleans Saints

Football, and scouting the sport, have been my life.

I've spent the last 26 years of my life scouting for five different NFL teams. Before that, I was a ball boy for the Chicago Bears from 1982-1987. I played college ball at Baylor University from 1988-1991 and coached college football for two years from 1992 to 1993 at North Texas State. So, in total, I've been around the game of football at either a college or professional level for the past 38 years. Like I said, football and scouting *are* my life!

My family ties in pro football run deep. My grandfather, Jim Parmer, was a longtime personnel man for the Chicago Bears and played professionally for the Eagles. My stepdad, E.J. Holub, played for the Kansas City Chiefs. I'm not sure I had much choice other than to somehow wind up in pro football. It is all my family talked about growing up.

At the age of 24, and after coaching at North Texas, I decided to change my career path and asked my grandfather about scouting. He immediately said I'd be a general manager before I was 40 because, in his opinion, "I had what it took to be successful in this business."

Four years later, I was able to prove him prophetic.

I became the GM of the Miami Dolphins, and for the next six years, I lived out my dream of running an NFL franchise. On one hand, I was proud to be the youngest GM in the NFL. On the other, I admit that I made some mistakes. The learning experience was the most invaluable of my career and has only made me a better scout, director and evaluator. I grew to understand that every decision you make affects the organization one way or another.

I first met Neil Stratton over the phone after I left the Dolphins in 2014. He connected me to a few influential agents who needed some advice on players, and he also helped put a few bucks in my pocket. It was after that conversation that I learned of his service, Inside the League, and that brief discussion with Neil has turned into a personal friendship. Professionally, he has been a great resource of information who I rely on several times a year during the course of our intense scouting season. His importance in our profession continues to grow, and I consider his work an asset for both the scouting and agent professions.

One of the more intriguing opportunities scouts experience in our profession is the wide scope of extreme personalities who we come in contact with in the football world. Whether it be the 32 billionaire owners to the hard-driving and extremely focused coaches to the aggressively eager scouts, if you've been in the business as long as I have, chances are you've almost seen it all! I say "almost" because just when you think you have seen and experienced it all, something brand new pops up and you have to make adjustments on the fly.

One of my favorite memories (but more frightening) experiences was in 2005 when I was with the Dallas Cowboys. I had recently been promoted to Vice President of College and Pro Scouting and was working on my first draft as one of the key decision-makers alongside owner Jerry Jones, his son, Stephen (the team's CEO and Executive Vice President) and head coach Bill Parcells. We had two first-round picks (Nos. 11 and 20) and Coach

Parcells and I were having a debate on the merits of Troy outside linebacker DeMarcus Ware and LSU defensive end. Marcus Spears.

Coach Parcells wanted to take Spears with the 11th pick. I loved Spears, too, but loved Ware just a little more because of his ability to rush the passer and, moreover, I felt that if we took Ware at 11, Spears would still be there at 20. It was the evening before the draft and Bill had left the office early as the proverbial hay was in the barn. Sometime after he left, the Joneses had asked for one last draft meeting with me and a few scouts to go over what our final thoughts were.

I laid out my plan that we should take Ware first and Spears at 20. Jerry asked me if Bill agreed. I explained that he liked both players but that, no, he didn't see it that way. He felt we needed to take Spears first. Jerry scoffed and said, "Well, you can tell him in the morning that we are taking Demarcus at 11, if he's there." As you can imagine, this was a lot easier said than done, as Bill left the office thinking he had won this argument and that we were taking Spears first. I knew this would not go over well!

Early the next morning, Bill walked in my office, and as I was just about to tell Bill of my discussions with the Joneses, Stephen walked in. "Jeff, did you tell him yet?," he asked. Bill just looked at me and half-yelled, "What?!"

"We're taking Ware at 11 because Jeff thinks we can get both players if we take Demarcus first," Stephen said.

Bill slammed his hand down on my desk. "No!! This is not what we are doing!!," he shouted. Staring deep into my soul, he asked, "Jeff, do you agree with this? I thought you were with me on this?"

I was crushed to go against him, but I knew I had to speak up and stand my ground.

"I'm with you, but I think we should take Ware first, and I am confident we'll get Spears at 20," I responded, calmly but firmly. "This is the only way we can get both players." Bill stormed out of my office and disappeared for the next three hours until about 30 minutes before the draft, when he came in with Jerry, laughing and smiling.

It turns out that we drafted Ware at 11, and for the next nine picks, I had that "heart in my throat" feeling. I knew that if I was right, Bill would celebrate my preparedness, but if I was wrong, I'd probably be fired. Or worse, Bill would not trust me anymore. Well, Spears was there at 20, and I smiled at Bill, expecting him to say something apologetic. All he would say was, "You're f___ lucky!" as he scowled and looked away. I smiled as if he just said "good job!" In a way, I think he did.

That ended up being one of the better drafts of my career. Outside of Ware and Spears, we took Tennessee linebacker Kevin Burnett in the second round, Minnesota running back Marion Barber III and Virginia defensive end Chris Canty in the fourth round; Ball State safety Justin Beriault and Pittsburgh offensive tackle Rob Petitti in the sixth round, and Auburn defensive tackle Jay Ratliff in the seventh. This draft helped catapult the Cowboys into the possession of one of the top defensive fronts, and best defenses, in the NFL for the next four years.

Fast-forward four years, and I'm the GM of the Dolphins and again working with Parcells. The year is 2008, and we had just signed QB Josh McCown to a free agent contract while drafting Michigan's Chad Henne in the second round as a developmental QB. Three weeks into training camp, and with two days left before our first preseason game, we literally couldn't get a first down against our defense. Then, out of the blue, the Jets cut Chad Pennington to make room for Brett Favre. Bill and I moved fast to sign him, and the transaction was announced the next morning.

Early that morning, Dolphins owner Wayne Huizenga called me, and it didn't take long to figure out he was not happy about the signing. In the course of ripping me, he asked me how I could make such a decision. If Pennington wasn't good enough for the Jets, he asked, what made him good enough for us? He was calm but blistered me with condescending questions without even allowing me to answer. To say the least, it was a good ass-chewing, delivered from likely the nicest man on the planet! Parcells said he would talk to Huizenga, but Mr H. and I didn't talk much the next four weeks.

Well, we rattled off about six wins in a row, including one against the Patriots in Foxboro, and Pennington was playing lights-out! I saw Mr H. on the sideline before the next game, and he approached me. "Boy, do I owe you an apology!," he said. "The next time I have an opinion, will you just tell me to mind my own business? Keep up the great work and keep me away from any football decisions!"

It was a small victory, but one I'll never forget. That 2008 team, with the help of Pennington, became the only one in NFL history to win 11 games following a year when they won only one. From 1-15 to 11-5. It was called one of the greatest turnarounds in NFL history.

A few years later, it was Draft Day 2017, and I was in my third year as the Assistant GM and Director of College Scouting for the Saints. For the second time in my career, I had two first-round picks, Nos. 11 and 32. We had 10 players on the board who we were considering at 11, with one being Texas Tech quarterback Patrick Mahomes. The draft started, and our own future Hall of Fame QB, Drew Brees, and two buddies walked in. They had been hog hunting and decided to swing by, asking to stick around for the first pick. I later learned that was the only time Drew ever came by the draft room on Draft Day.

After about seven picks, we had three players still on the board who we wanted, with one being Mahomes. The tension in the room was mounting as everyone in the room but Drew knew that we might be drafting his successor. I whispered to our Executive Vice President and GM, Mickey Loomis, that someone needed to tell Drew what he might soon be witnessing. Head coach Sean Payton finally took Drew up to the board and explained to him what might happen. To his credit, Drew was calm and understood, but it was a very awkward moment.

After nine picks, there were still three players on the board who we really liked. We knew we had Ohio State cornerback Marshon Lattimore or Mahomes if we stayed put. Soon thereafter, the Chiefs jumped in front of us and picked Mahomes. So, we drafted Lattimore, who became the 2017 NFL Defensive Rookie of the Year.

The drama wasn't over that day, though, as we still had the 32nd pick. One of our objectives in this draft was to help the defense, but we didn't have a defensive player who met our standards at 32. Alabama linebacker Reuben Foster was enticing, especially to Sean, but due to some outside concerns, Foster was no lock to be our next selection. Still, Sean was intrigued, and at pick 29 or 30, he decided to call Foster personally. Neither Mickey nor I knew what was Sean's intention exactly, but we knew Sean was on a mission.

We still had another player high on our board, Wisconsin offensive tackle Ryan Ramcyzk, who we would have considered at pick 11. At that point, I was convinced we were taking Ramcyzk – until Sean called Foster. To this day, I am still not sure who we would've taken if Foster had not been taken by San Francisco the pick before ours. We've never discussed it. In fact, we already had Ramcyzk's name filled out on the draft card and just turned it in with very little discussion, like we all knew this was the player we were taking all along. It turned out that Ramcyzk was an outstanding pick, but there's that "what if" attached to this pick that keeps you thinking.

One more story from the 2017 draft. This one involves our pre-draft trip to visit defensive end Derek Barnett, running back Alvin Kamara, cornerback Cam Sutton and quarterback Josh Dobbs at the University of Tennessee. Our owners, Tom and Gayle Benson, generously allowed Sean, a few coaches and I to use their private plane to fly around to some pro days and workouts.

This particular visit was memorable. We had dinner with all four players, but Kamara was our target. I wanted Sean to get to know him as best he could, so I sat him next to Alvin. Sean fell in love instantly.

The next morning, I sat in the QB room along with our offensive coordinator, Pete Carmichael, as well as Dobbs and Kamara. Alvin knew the offense as well as Dobbs, who is highly intelligent in the film room and is now a backup in Jacksonville. At any rate, the only thing left was to see Alvin run a few routes for Sean, and if he performed well, I knew we would move heaven and earth to get him.

Well, later that morning, I'm on the indoor field waiting for Alvin and the rest of the players to get dressed, and Alvin finds me. He told me he wouldn't be working out and that his agent had advised him to sit out and not get hurt. This was not good, because I knew how much Sean wanted to see him move around. I calmly advised Alvin that he needed to run a few routes for the head coach. I told him that we didn't get on a private plane to Knoxville just to take him to dinner, that we'd come to see him move around.

I leveled with him, telling him that one of two things were about to happen. One, he could sit out, and Sean would be frustrated by his poor decision and failure to understand the situation before him. Sean would likely be pissed at me, and worst of all, we would leave Knoxville with the feeling that we could take him or leave him.

The second option would be for him to find some cleats upstairs and run a few routes for the coach. If all went well, Payton would be happy, we would all be fired up to draft him, and we would find a way to get him on our team. Alvin's response: "Can you give me five minutes to find some cleats?"

The maturity Alvin showed with this situation was unreal. It made us fall in love with him even more because of the way he handled it. He went on to crush the workout, and we later gave up next year's second-round choice to move up and draft Alvin. The 2017 draft was historic for the Saints as Lattimore and Kamara became the defensive and offensive rookies of the year – only the second time in 50 years that players from the same team received those honors. We actually won Inside the League's inaugural award for having the best draft, and I accepted the trophy from Neil at the 2018 combine.

As you're reading this book, whether for entertainment or for education, I can assure you that the people telling these stories have traveled more miles, stayed in more hotels away from their families, have typed up more reports and have more passion toward their craft than most. These men are my brothers, and we all share the love of football and the passion for finding the next great one. I believe you all will enjoy...

CHAPTER 1
So you want to be a scout? 10 things to know

W hen I launched Inside the League in 2002, my goals were the same as anyone who launches a business: fame and fortune, but short of that, at least the chance to raise my family comfortably while pursuing my passion. But here was my secret dream: to figure out the objective standards teams use to select the best players. What *really* matters to scouts? What is the secret sauce that all teams seek? What do the best teams know that the bad teams don't?

Twenty years later, I'm still seeking answers to all those questions. However, I have made a few observations. Here are a few of them.

1.Throw out all rules. No matter what any scout says, there are none. As a fan, or as a young football professional, you will be told certain positions have to be certain sizes, run certain speeds, or have certain production. Maybe, maybe not. Scouting is, was and always will be *highly subjective*. Trends, popularity, which players are deemed to be "safe" at what rounds, etc., matter far more to most teams and their scouts than they'd like to admit. But none of that matters because . . . .

2. There are very few secrets among scouts. Groupthink is a *major* part of NFL evaluation, if for no other reason than self-preservation. Former Rams area scout Danton Barto tells the story of a scout who stumbled on a talented player in the Southwest Athletic Conference (SWAC) who wasn't a preseason prospect. The scout called Barto and told him he needed to know about this player and that he should make sure to check him out on his tour of the Southeast. Keep in mind that Danton's friend didn't tell him what round he expected the player to go in; he just told him there was a player he needed to make sure not to miss. This is pretty common; scouts who travel the same regions tend to get pretty chummy. Often, as they climb the ladder, they hire the scouts they befriended on the road.

3. No matter what teams say, there are players on the street who could make NFL rosters. Even when scouts are sharing the players they like and helping out their buddies, there are still players who slip through the cracks. It's a measure of teams' reliance on BLESTO and National Football Scouting. Most scouts make out their fall travel schedules based on the players the two scouting services say are the best prospects. If you are a small-school player who isn't at least identified as a player of interest by one of the two scouting services, you are at a major disadvantage. This is especially true if you live in an area that isn't dense with football-playing schools. You often see sleepers come out of the Northwest or Western plains; this is one reason North Dakota State's Carson Wentz entered his senior season projected as a seventh-round pick or undrafted free agent.

4. Scouts work extremely hard – but also take shortcuts. No scout sees every school, talks to every coach, watches game film of every school. What's more, some NFL teams are a bit lenient on their scouts and don't require that they file their reports promptly. This lends itself to varying clarity on different players or an overreliance on what a friendly coach or fellow scout said about the player.

5. It's fun to look back at draft busts, but the truth is that most players are drafted about where everyone else would have picked them. Yes, the Raiders look dumb for taking LSU's

JaMarcus Russell over Georgia Tech's Calvin Johnson, but the truth is that many teams, maybe even most, would have done the same thing. By the same token, every scout knows a story about a team that was desperate to pick Player A, missed out, and settled on Player B, only to watch Player A bust and Player B become a star.

6. There is a general consensus among scouts on almost every player. You will be told that certain teams draft better than others, and they do. Still, bottom line, teams generally agree on which players get a pass based on size/speed/character/injury questions; which players are Day 1, Day 2 and Day 3; which players' upsides are the requisite to be worthy of being drafted high, regardless of their on-field production, etc. One scout texted me this when the coronavirus quarantines wiped out March workouts at schools: "Pro days are when everyone huddled and picked one another's brains."

7. At the same time, there are players who fall every year and virtually no one knows why. Often, players will have a comparably minor injury issue, or an arrest, or something else that makes them less sexy. They often fall not a round or two, but completely out of the draft. Several scouts have told me they watched a player get passed over round after round and wound up doing the same, simply because they were convinced everyone else knew something they didn't know.

8. Teams always brag about taking the best player available, but most of the time they take the best player available where they have the most pressing need. Go back through the draft virtually every year, and you'll find that most teams took players in the early rounds where they had demonstrated weaknesses. This is one reason why so many first-round quarterbacks go bust.

They were never first-round talents, but a team was hoping to capture lightning in a bottle.

9. Quarterback is the No. 1 position where players are most often over-drafted, and there is no No. 2. This will probably always be true. It's such a high-impact position that if you have a need, and you hit, you can change your team's fortunes practically overnight. At the same time, quarterbacks are the toughest players to evaluate, and guesswork is an almost accepted part of the sorting-out process. There's a reason Brady, Montana and Brees weren't first-rounders, but Schlichter, Marinovich and Couch were.

Let me expand on this a bit. A couple years ago, I had a conversation with one scout who I thought best explained the quarterback predicament. He said scouts were all over the place on California QB Jared Goff, with some liking his upside, and others seeing him as comparable to Memphis' Paxton Lynch and even Mississippi State's Dak Prescott. These scouts preferred North Dakota State's Carson Wentz. Despite Wentz's small-school pedigree, they liked his intangibles and the multiple national titles he was part of at NDSU.

These scouts also had concerns that Goff had gone from nowhere as a sophomore to a possible No. 1 overall as a junior. They just didn't feel his total body of work justified the investment.

"That's a concern when you're taking a guy first overall, with a lot of (varied) grades," my friend said.

I'd agree. Teams have to make the best decision based on the information they have, and obviously opinions vary. However, if Goff turns out to be a guy who doesn't live up to expectations, it could be because the Rams felt they had to have a quarterback, and he looked like their best option. The one resounding message I get back from scouts is that the surest way to miss on a pick is to draft based on need and not purely on the best player available.

Once again, there's still plenty of time for Goff to turn into Aaron Rodgers. No one knows what the future holds. That's what makes the draft so intriguing.

10. Beauty is *always* in the eye of the beholder. To illustrate this point, consider this story:

In January 2008, Wake Forest LB Aaron Curry was considering entering the draft as a junior. As most top prospects do, Curry put in for his draft projection with the NFL's College Advisory Committee. He received a third-round grade. For what it's worth, the top five picks in the draft were Michigan OT Jake Long (Dolphins), Virginia DE Chris Long (Rams), Boston College QB Matt Ryan (Falcons), Arkansas running back Darren McFadden (Raiders) and LSU DT Glenn Dorsey (Chiefs). Two linebackers went in the first round that year – Southern Cal's Keith Rivers (No. 9 to Cincinnati) and Tennessee's Jerod Mayo (No. 10 to New England), while Oklahoma's Curtis Lofton (more of a pure inside linebacker) went No. 37 overall to the Falcons.

Based at least partially on that projection, Curry chose to stay in school.

The draft came and went, and then a couple weeks later, National Football Scouting, one of the two services that grades players for subscribing NFL teams, listed him as *the No. 1-rated player for the '09 draft*. National usually meets with teams around the Memorial Day weekend, so this was *literally weeks* after the '08 draft. In other words, the College Advisory Committee (CAC) said there were about 100 players in the '08 draft who were better than any player in the '09 draft.

All 32 NFL teams are represented on the CAC, as well as National and BLESTO. In the space of three to four months – during which no football was played – the opinions of one group of professional football evaluators determined Curry was a third-rounder, while another group of scouts said he could be the No. 1 pick in the draft.

As a postscript, National was right. Curry went No. 4 in '09 to the Seahawks.

Draftable or undraftable?

Ask your average NFL draft fan, and he'll say that all teams see players about the same way. I agree, though it's not entirely true. I think there's also a perception that every team forms ratings on 250 players, one through 250, in a similar form to the draft itself. Not true as well. Most teams start by evaluating 2,000 players heading into the season and reduce that number to about 150-180 draftable players on draft day. Whittling that number down is done differently across the NFL. Some teams wind up with far fewer than 150 players with draftable grades.

For example, some teams (Dallas and New England, especially) have higher risk tolerance. These teams are more likely to keep a Randy Gregory, for example, on their board even though the then-Nebraska defensive end had a roomful of red flags related to his drug issues. On the other hand, I once spoke to a GM who interviewed Gregory before the draft, and he applauded him for "getting naked" about his drug issues at Nebraska. The GM *still* took him off his team's board.

Then there's injury issues. If a player had surgeries on his knees, ankles, hamstring or anything from the waist down, he's in trouble, especially if he's a ball carrier who's going to take a lot of punishment. I don't have a rule of thumb for when such injuries are fatal draft-wise, but injuries are a real factor in the draft process.

Now let's look at performance. If a player is a college teammate of a player rated as draft-worthy by either National or BLESTO, then his film is in the NFL's dub (film) center. That means there's a better chance someone has seen him and perhaps taken an interest in him.

If a player (a) doesn't have any character red flags, (b) hasn't suffered a series of major injuries, and (c) has been seen by NFL teams –plus he comes from an FBS school and is at least 6-feet tall – he will improve his chances of having the maximum number of teams view him positively. Obviously height varies as a differentiator for different positions, but you get the picture.

CHAPTER 2
Building the foundation

Before we go any further, let's discuss the differences in the types of scouts (forgive me if you already know this).

A "pro scout" evaluates players who are post-draft and typically have already played in the league (or who *are* playing in the league). These are the evaluators that teams rely on in free agency and injury replacements. They are mostly in-house and don't travel the nation from August until November (though they are often called on to help out with pro days in March and April). Until recently, pro scouts were mostly older scouts who were less highly regarded by the NFL community, though that line is starting to be erased as more and more talented college scouts are rewarded with "pro" jobs to get them off the road.

A "college scout" is what most people have in mind when they think of the word. These are the guys who crisscross the country every fall, trying to hit every school where there might be a prospect. Also known as area scouts, they tend to cover one region of the country. Most often, these regions are the Southeast, Northeast, East, Southwest, Midwest, Midlands (generally, the states between Kansas and California), Northwest or West, but no two teams cut up the nation the same way. Most often, these scouts try to see every school with a prospect – usually those designated as such by BLESTO or National Football Scouting (more on them later). Area scouts are cross-checked by national scouts, who are themselves typically cross-checked by a team's Director of College Scouting or assistant director, then the Director of Player Personnel or an assistant. In this way, though it goes against common perception, no single scout is specifically responsible for "finding" a player. It's true an area scout might identify a player who no one else knew about, as Chicago Bears area scout Sam Summerville is credited with doing for running back Tarik Cohen. However, no team pulls the trigger on a player on Draft Day unless four or five other scouts have signed off on him.

With respect to salaries, there's no definite pay scale. Almost every scout is on a two-year deal; that's standard. If you're a scouting intern or assistant, you're making McDonald's money. I was asked for a referral a couple years ago for a job that paid $15 an hour in a city that is extremely expensive. Even though the team promised plenty of overtime (I have no doubt that's true), the person I referred eventually withdrew from the process. He was in his late 20s and just didn't want to return to the bottom of the pay scale.

Veteran scouts call scouting assistants "20/20 guys," i.e., in their early 20s and making around $20,000. That's not exactly true these days, however. We began conducting a salary survey among active scouts in 2018. Our most recent numbers (2020) showed that about a third of scouts with five years or less experience earn $50,000-$65,000 per year. Not bad, presuming you're fresh out of college, don't mind spending most of your life in a hotel and living on an expense account, and have designs on running your own scouting staff one day.

If you look at scouts with six to10 years of experience, almost half (44 percent) are making $100,000 or more. By the time scouts get to 10 years in, virtually everyone is making $125,000 or more. Scouts are regularly frustrated with their level of pay. My experience has been that they see assistant coaches as their easiest comparison, and coaches are making four or five times what scouts are making. So, there's often friction.

Is it possible to prepare in college for a scouting job?

It's becoming more common for scouts to have sports management degrees. Also, more and more NFL evaluators are graduating from Ivy League schools with degrees in finance, economics or math. There's a perception that you can go to an online academy or specialized school to get a leg up. I won't argue that some of these courses are good – many are taught or led by friends of mine with years in the business – but I see them more as an extra layer of qualification rather than the key that turns the lock.

The truth is, most people who are hired into scouting did it because of their network. They worked around the game for a few years, winning friends and impressing the right people. Many of them found mentors who would go to bat aggressively for them. This is what used to be called "paying your dues." Unfortunately, there are always some who will skip a few steps on the way through connections or nepotism, but to me, there's still no substitute for working your way up.

Just get in

Now another little story. When I was 26 in the mid-1990s, I found out the Saints -- I'm a big New Orleans fan -- had an opening for a media intern. At the time, I was working as a sports reporter for a tiny newspaper. I knew someone who was leaving the internship to go somewhere else, and the team had an opening. I really wanted to do it. I was born in South Louisiana about the same time as when the Saints were born. I got an interview, and I had a house I was going to live in and everything. Anyway, after I interviewed, the Saints called and said, "Hey, sorry, we can't do it. But we have a business internship if you want to come and sell tickets."

Today, I think, what if I had gone and done it? They were going to pay me a stipend of about $500 per month. Even back then, I don't know how I would have lived. I would have basically been calling people at home and working on commission selling tickets. Back then, I thought, I'm a media guy. I'm not going to do that. But if you want to cut your teeth and get inside the building, sometimes that's the way you have to do it. I can't emphasize it enough: get any kind of role with the team. Once you're there, it's so much easier to get an introduction. It's like you've been made official when you get inside. Even if you're sweeping floors, if you can get inside the building, you are halfway home. That's especially true when it comes to landing a scouting role.

No experience necessary

When ITL started, identifying scouts was the easiest thing to do in the world. They all had gray hair, if they had any hair at all. They were often very heavy. Most of the time they were college coaches who had never made it to head coach … or maybe they did, and they got tired and didn't want to recruit anymore … or they just had buddies who worked for NFL teams. They came in and worked for four or five years to get a pension, then rode off into the football sunset, so to speak. They had probably worked in one area of the country primarily, so they had a good network already, and they had developed an eye, so they knew talent.

It was a good way to hire a scout, and for a team, it was worth it because team managers knew they were getting a return on their investment. Importantly, however, these scouts were expected to know who the players were in their area.

Now, because the Patriots have been successful, everyone wants to follow their model. This model is to employ young and inexperienced scouts who obtain hard facts, i.e., measures (height and weight); arrest record and disposition of the arrests; anything about suspensions; and anything about what the guys at the office say about the players. However, the team doesn't want an opinion on who's draftable, per se. That's left to the team's senior evaluators and upper management. This is one reason you don't have to have an evolved scouting eye. To some degree, you're often a glorified errand boy if you're a scouting assistant.

The Modern NFL Scouting Department

So how is the modern scouting department made? What slots need to be filled to have a successful operation?

To answer that question, I looked at the 12 teams who qualified for the NFL playoffs in 2017. I sought out the common thread between the Patriots, Steelers, Jaguars, Chiefs, Titans and Bills in the AFC, plus the Eagles, Vikings, Rams, Saints, Panthers and Falcons in the NFC. First off, I have to reduce the teams under the microscope to 11 as the Panthers neither published their scouts and their assignments on their website nor published a media guide with that information. So, I took a look at the other teams.

GM stability: This is a really hard factor to measure. There were teams in the playoffs like the Patriots and Saints that, technically, have had the same GM in place for the last two decades. While New England's Bill Belichick is in a class by himself and not your typical GM, New Orleans' Mickey Loomis is not your traditional, in-charge-on-draft-day kind of GM. The fortunes of the Saints didn't really turn around until Assistant GM Jeff Ireland was hired. In fact, if there's a trend, it's movement away from centralized decision-making as several of the GMs in the playoffs last year either had their personnel power stripped or haven't been around long enough to really be judged (entering the 2018 season, for example, Buffalo's Brandon Beane and Kansas City's Brett Veach had been on the job two years or less).

Director-level scouts and executives: How many of these teams are loaded with chiefs and are less-needful of Indians? There's no real consensus, but it seems that less is more. The Patriots, a team that's got most of its power in a tight circle around Belichick, had just three director-level members on its scouting staff in 2018. So did the Titans, led by former Patriots executive Jon Robinson. The Bills, Vikings, Saints and Steelers each had four. On the other end of the spectrum were the Jaguars and Eagles with seven each.

Total scouts: Again, no team defines every evaluator the same way. However, when counting actual "scouts" in the 11 front offices — not people who are managing and making decisions, but those who are doing base-level evaluation of players — the magic number seems to be 10. The Steelers, Rams, Titans, Jaguars and Bills all had 10 members on their staffs who seemed to be primarily scouts; the Vikings had 11. On the other end of the spectrum, the NFC champion Eagles had six and the Chiefs had eight.

New challenges, new benefits

One of the best things about working with people in the game is that you get to ask them questions that demystify one of the most intriguing jobs in the game of football, at least in my opinion. When you ask about things that go a deeper than what's normally asked by the media, you get interesting answers.

I was curious about how the job of being a scout has evolved, and whether the changes have been positive ones, so I asked several friends in the scouting community this question: Do you think it's harder (more schools to cover, entitled players, troublesome agents, greater media involvement) or easier (digital age, easier communications, better medical data, pro days more efficient) to be a scout than it was 10 years ago?

About a dozen scouts, some on the area level and some higher-ups, responded. Here's what they told me:

- "I wouldn't say it is easier or harder, but it is different. Fans are more knowledgeable about the process and media coverage is more intense, but instant access to video, social media, and more advanced draft studies are among the changes for the better."

- "Easier, mostly due to video – VHS tapes, then DVDs, now all digital. (Previously) we'd have to wait for tapes or DVDs from NFL video, then team video, always late. Now we can access any game the next week, all on a (Microsoft) Surface. Also, background info on the internet is easier."

- "(The) digital age (has) made it easy to watch the game tape and write reports, but you still have to watch the tape and write the reports to have a great draft!"

- "Tough to say, but I would (say) it was harder travel-wise 10 years ago because I'm sure there was less communication, marginal GPS services and specified roles in colleges."

- "Easier, because the internet allows you to get background info or stats instantly. That can also be a negative if you have lazy scouts. Fifteen years ago, a scout would actually have to make a school visit to watch film. Now, you get it on your iPad or computer immediately."

CHAPTER 3
Getting the job

T he bulk of the work done evaluating players for the NFL Draft is done by area scouts, the warriors of the profession. At Inside the League, we spend a lot of time telling their stories and trying to make their jobs a little easier with our salary survey, helping out with pro days in March and anything else.

To that end, we decided to review a four-year range of hiring and firing in the scouting world to see where scouts came from, as well as what's happening to the people who hold that title. The question we sought to answer is, where are area scouts coming from these days? The perception is that older, more seasoned evaluators are no longer en vogue, and that there's a definite shelf life for old-school college scouts. But what do the numbers say?

We counted 90 NFL personnel professionals who took a job as area scouts between 2015 and 2019 (college side only, not pro scout). Here's what we found.

- For 70 scouts, achieving area scout was a clear promotion. Almost half (31) were promoted from scouting assistant, which has become the most common way teams hire college evaluators.

- Eighteen were combine scouts (BLESTO or NFS), probably the second-most common route.

- Eleven were in pro roles or assisted on both the pro and college side.

- Four other scouts moved over from the pro side. All four were young scouts who were most likely being promoted, though it's unclear if they received a bump in pay. Either way, probably good news for young scouts.

- Three more came from non-NFL scouting services, though it's important to note that two of the three had extensive pro football backgrounds and weren't plucked capriciously from #DraftTwitter.

- Another two hopped directly from other leagues (the CFL and Arena League) into area roles.

- One was a college scouting coordinator who was sent on the road.

- One moved over from the coaching side.

Another note: these trends are representative of what's happened the last five years. At least 10 new area scouts have been hired from within every year since 2015 (not counting 2020 of course). In 2017, 22 (!) were elevated from scouting assistant and combine scout roles.

Of course, it wasn't all good news for new area scouts. We identified 17 of the 90 who were taking a step down from national scout or a director-level position, presumably after a period of unemployment. Bottom line, the overwhelming majority of new area scout hires (81 percent) were people with limited experience who were promoted from within.

We also counted 148 area scouts over the same time period (2015-2019) who experienced a change in job status. The news for these experienced evaluators was not as positive. What do the numbers say?

About a third (54) saw a negative change in status, which we defined as a termination without rehire; acceptance of a lesser job (most often a move to combine scout or college scouting coordinator with another team); exit for another league (CFL, XFL, AAF) or all-star game (Senior Bowl, NFLPA Collegiate Bowl), most often after a termination; or departure for a college personnel job (again, most likely after a termination).

Another 38 changed teams or changed areas, but remained as area scouts. Presumably, there was no accompanying raise for any of these jobs. Another six switched to the pro side, which, again, likely did not come with a direct change in salary.

We counted 50 who climbed the ladder. Of the 50, 21 took a director- or assistant director-level post, and 27 took a national scout or regional cross-checker role. Two others moved to the coaching side, which is typically more lucrative.

Here's where things get a little alarming, especially if you're a veteran scout. Of the 50 evaluators moving up since 2015, 34 were promoted before 2018. Last year? Just six promotions. This year – an anomaly, sure, but still – we've seen more negative trends for area scouts as three have been let go, along with a regional scout. None were promoted.

Maybe better days are ahead. Maybe the 2021 offseason will bring a return to 2017 conditions, when we saw 18 area scouts get bumped into director or national roles. We'll see if trends turn around this time next year.

Origin Stories

After I get to know a scout, I always try to learn about how he got into scouting. Learning how others have made it into the game is a great way to figure out if you can do the same. The following are the stories of several current and former scouts and how they got into the game.

Barto only did one three-year stint as an area scout with the Rams, but he says it was the fulfillment of a lifelong dream of reaching the NFL. That doesn't mean the job didn't come with drawbacks.

"It was an interesting dynamic there at the Rams, because Coach (Jeff) Fisher was the guy that ran the team basically. (GM) Les (Snead) facilitated -- it was a good relationship -- but you felt that (in that) building was a very weird feeling-out process between what's going on. I think with me, it was a unique thing, because Coach Dave McGinnis, and Coach Fisher realized I just wanted to do football work, and I learned how we did things there, our way, the way they wanted them done. I was lucky.

"Les sent me down to the draft. He said, 'Do you want a job? And . . . I got a kid in high school. I don't want to move. What do I have to do? What does that mean? And Les said, well, Dan, you don't got to move. We're going to give you a territory. I had a weird territory, probably that nobody on other teams in the NFL ever had. I did Arkansas, Tennessee, Kentucky, Mississippi and Alabama. That was my area, and he said, 'let's do it for a year,' and I said, OK, I'm game. Let's try this out for a year.

"Then Les set the first contract in front of my face, and I was like, 'Oh, like, no.' I mean, I was like, 'no, I can't do it for this.' You kind of have to swallow your pride, honestly, if you want to be in the NFL. And I did. I mean, when I signed, I took a big pay cut. It was a big one, and I wasn't used to that, but I said, 'I want to be in the NFL.' And for me to be in the NFL . . . everybody has their different reason. For me, I never got there as a football player, and it was kind of something that I needed for myself to prove to myself that I belonged in that building. It was an opportunity to do something that I always wanted to prove to myself. It had nothing to do with anything else. So I got that opportunity. I was always just (thrilled) about getting that opportunity. Then as time went on, it grew. First year went well, and they asked me to come back, and I came back again, re-upped."

***

Bob Morris has scouted with the Browns and 49ers, serving under Trent Baalke (San Francisco) and Phil Savage (Cleveland). Bob's story of getting into scouting is very much akin to what you saw commonly in the 1990s and early 2000s, i.e., former college coaches in the third or fourth quarters of their careers who were looking to channel their contacts and experience in a different direction.

"My son had me do this book thing on writing your life, and he asked me, what are some of the most unexpected, or crazy, things that have happened to you? I think getting fired (as an assistant coach) at Akron was one of them, because I just didn't see it happening. Not by a letter by FedEx while I'm on vacation. So that's in January, and so I sent out a bunch of resumes. I'm 45 years old . . . and experienced, probably a little too experienced for my own good at times. I had spent 13 or 14 years in the Big 10, and just found it really tough to find a coaching job at that time.

"I tried to reinvent myself as a special teams/tight end coach, and didn't really get past sending a resume, to be honest with you. My wife wanted to get me out of the house; I was under foot. I knew (former Colts head coach) Chuck Pagano because I played with Chuck's dad in high school, and Chuck had been the secondary coach for Butch Davis of Miami, (and a year before), I was supposed to go down there for an interview, but that didn't happen. It didn't happen because Butch Davis took the job in Cleveland (as head coach of the Browns). So Butch gets there, he's there for a year, and he doesn't like the scouting staff – it's just a bunch of numbers guys and a bunch of evaluators that hadn't played football. I called Chuck just to go up to mini-camp. Chuck called me back and said, 'hey, we're looking for some scouts. We want to change things over. Would you mind interviewing for that job when you come up here?' I said, 'no, I don't mind.' That's nothing in my wildest dreams I thought I would do. Always, scouts were coming through my office and talking to me about guys at Indiana and Akron, and I never even thought that's what I would do. Never really wanted to do it.

"But I go up and see Chuck, meet with Phil Neri, who was (Director of College Scouting) at the time, and he gives me a film to watch. We go out to practice, and he asks me what I think about the film, and then asked me some questions about the (film), and there really wasn't much of an interview. I met with Butch Davis, and Butch tells me what he's looking for, and he needs a guy that can tell him what the hell a 4-3, 3-technique is going to do – is he going to get up the field? Is he going to close? – and he's tired of just the personnel guy, a height/weight/speed guy and that stuff. I said, 'I can do that.' So, I got the job, and I was lucky, because they were looking for a scout on the road with coach's eyes. And that's really been my role in every NFL room

I've been in, is I'm kind of the coach's eyes in a room with other scouts. It especially helps with the secondary. That's kind of been my expertise through the years. So, I get the job with Cleveland.

"(Before getting let go in Cleveland), I kind of knew that was happening, and so I had made myself pretty visible during the all-star games. I can remember being at the East-West game -- that's (in 2008) when Joe Flacco was down there -- and Trent Baalke was there. He was the interim GM for the 49ers at that time. I was at the combine, and Trent was sitting there with the other San Francisco coaches, and as I went by, I just made it a point to sit down and talk to him. I had been in some rooms with Trent, and had never worked for him, but I knew that he was in a situation where he was the interim GM and could get the GM job. He didn't know (if he would), I didn't know, but I got let go back in Cleveland, so I called Trent, and said, 'hey, look, I figure this is going to happen.' It did, and I had a job within 23 hours. Trent told me the reason I had a job . . . wasn't because of who had called him -- I had a couple of those -- but because of the guys I had worked with on the road that he respected. He asked them about me, and the way I worked, and that's what got me the job. I passed that on to a lot of the young guys when I got to Cleveland. As I was leaving, I said, 'hey guys, I'm out of this job, but I got another job because of the way I acted on the road.'"

***

For Cowboys College Scouting Coordinator Chris Hall, it was a matter of being in the right place at the right time – as well as taking a chance on a man that wasn't very popular at the time.

"I moved around (growing up). My dad worked for an oil company, so I moved around every three or four years to a different place. I think that helped me as an adult, having to make new friends as a kid and everything, to be open to change and that sort of thing. You will find, in this business, as you go, a lot of it's your personality and how you get along with other people. I ended up at SMU. This is back when you actually had newspapers you read every morning instead of everything digital. I was the kid that looked up the box score every day, whether it was baseball or football, to see who had stats, who was making plays. I read and absorbed all that information that I could.

"When I got to SMU, my thing there was, I got into the whole intramural program. I ended up, by the time I was done, I was one of the students in charge. That was everything from setting up schedules to putting officials with the games and everything from basketball to volleyball to soccer to softball. It was a great way to make extra money in school. You pay yourself to ref and supervise at the same time. I was making 13 bucks an hour back then, which was pretty good. It handled beer money and stuff like that, so it was good. But when I left SMU, I graduated with an advertising degree, and my minor is (physical education), whatever they called it back then. There (weren't) sports management degrees.

"Anyhow, I had my big advertising degree, and I didn't have a job when I graduated. I was living with some friends, and one of my buddies, he got a job with the Dallas Cowboys in the public relations department as an intern. He'd been there for a year, and he calls me up August of 1990, and he says, 'They just let this guy go in the scouting department out there. Is that something you'd be interested in?' I'm thinking, I've got about 500 bucks left in my bank account. I'm going to have to move back home with mom and dad if I don't get a real job. And he helped me set up an interview out there. I got a second interview, and I got hired in September of 1990. That was a year after Jerry Jones had bought the team, and he had let go of Tom Landry and was the most hated guy in Dallas at the time for firing Tom Landry and bringing Jimmy Johnson in, and the whole bit. Within five years, we won three Super Bowls in the early '90s. We didn't know any better."

***

Falcons national scout Phil Emery has had a fascinating career in scouting, serving as GM of the Bears from 2012-14 and scouting for the Bears and Chiefs, as well as having two stints in Atlanta. I narrowly missed him during my time at the U.S. Naval Academy; he came in as the football team's strength coach as I was leaving. Phil was kind enough to speak at the 2015 ITL Combine Seminar shortly after he was let go in Chicago. He had some incredible insights on breaking into the business.

"We all have a unique story, OK? Here are three things that I've learned, that stick with me in the journey that I've had. One: anything is possible. It doesn't matter what your background is. Like I said, everyone has their unique one. My dad is a GM factory worker. My mom is the best waitress in the United States, and she did that for 21 years. Then she decided to be a factory worker for another 10. So, I came from a blue-collar background. Other people come from less fortunate (backgrounds); other people come from much more fortunate ones. It isn't about where you come from. It's about having goals, and deciding that anything is possible to get where you want to go.

"(The) second thing it took me until I was about 30 to figure out is, it's about others, it's not about yourself. So, figure out a way to do it for the benefit of others and you will have a lot more fun. We all chase the dollar to an extent, because we want to feed our family, we want to provide for them and we want them to have a higher standard of living. You're going to do that quicker if you serve others first. It'll come a lot faster for you. You reap what you sow.

"The third thing is, take risks, and don't be afraid of them, OK? I'm sure there's very few people in here that have talked to the one-percenters, the top one percent of wealthy people in the United States. I'm not one of those. I didn't come from there. If you are, you're very fortunate. You probably took risks to get there. Take risks. I reminded myself when I got the job in Chicago (that) you've never really had anything, so swing harder. Don't choke up on the bat. I swung hard. It didn't work out, but I'm proud of one thing: we weren't afraid to swing. Nobody left me at the plate looking at the ball. We spent every dime we could spend, and we tried to make the best decisions that we could.

"So that's my advice. Remember: anything is possible, do it for the benefit of others and don't be afraid to take risks. The more risks you take, the more change will happen in your life, and ultimately change makes you stronger.

"We rejected some people in Kansas City that ended up working for me in Chicago. Why? They took our advice. One young man who is now a combine scout we told, 'hey, you need to go get some experience.' So what he did, he was volunteering at Indiana in their video department, and he went and became a small college coach for two years. Then he still had a passion to come back and work for less for an NFL club as a scouting assistant. That is the path, OK?

"I will tell you that (in) the interview process for interns, there are important things that people are looking for. It's like any profession: work ethic, demonstrated work output, intelligence, humbleness, body language, eye contact, handshake. For some reason, men have a tendency to let their guard down, and they show a little bit more of their true selves (more) with women than they do with the men that they're interviewing with. So, we always went back to (women around the office) and said, 'what do you think?' And they were usually the more accurate persons in the building in terms of hiring those folks in those types of positions, those entry-level scouting assistants, salary cap assistants, whatever. It was a big help.

"I'll give you a couple hints in terms of things that I'm looking for. One thing that always was a turn-off, and I might as well stop the interview, when somebody told me they wanted to be GM. For somebody to walk in that's 25, 26, 27 years old, and has very little work experience, and the thing they want to tell you about their goals is they want to be GM, that sounds great, but what I wanted to hear was that they had a passion, to do whatever we ask, and to excel in their role, and then grow from there. That's really important. That was our whole thing in the building is, seeking excellence in your role, and then you'll get more. We all have that goal, that we want to get to the top of something. However, that's not necessarily the thing to share when you have very little experience. It's almost like you're, to me, almost belittling those people that are between that job and your job, that you're going to go from here to there. You've got to take the steps, and I want to make sure that whoever took those jobs understood those steps were a requirement. That humbleness and work ethic and pride in your work were a requirement for advancement. Not just being a good guy with a good smile. That never is enough.

"To be considered a full work week, to get a 40-hour work week, that pay has to start about $25,000 to $30,000 for the (team's) labor people to file (for the government's minimum standards). So, our scouting assistants, our beginning-level scouting assistants, our salary cap assistants, we had a lot of people to kind of fill in that category. They all start at about $31,000. So how do you get to that job? Well, because it pays, there's going to be a requirement. We wanted experience. This was true when I was in Kansas City, and this was true when I was in Chicago as a GM. We're looking for at least two years. Now if that's in scouting, we're looking for you to have two years' experience at some level -- small college, high school -- and actively being involved in the game of football.

"We've gotten some unbelievable (applicant) letters. Like, 'I've been an analyst for Morgan Stanley for the last 20 years, but my true passion is football, and I'll come work for you for free, and I'd love you to hire me, and this is what I bring.' Well, I always looked it as, if your passion is football, at some point you wouldn't have started after 20 years, OK? If your passion is football, it's going to start a lot earlier. So, you need to take that into consideration, and those that you advise wanting to get into the game, have them get into the game at some level.

"When I was at Kansas City, and at my time here in Chicago, we rejected a lot of people that we actually interviewed because we just didn't feel like they were ever going to get where they needed to go just doing exactly what we asked them to do. They didn't have enough under the belt to do the job we were looking for, and your lack of preparation for that job is going to affect it down the road."

***

Blake Beddingfield spent about two decades with the Titans, last serving as the team's Director of College Scouting before Jon Robinson arrived as GM and brought in his own people. Beddingfield has become a true friend and an invaluable part of Inside the League. He is my top author of scouting reports for ITL clients, and he's also spoken, at my request, at multiple events. The following is one story he tells about his entry into the business.

"I had a general manager that was a mentor of mine 20 years ago before I got in the NFL, and he told me, 'Blake, I know of an organization that's hiring. Be persistent with the person that's doing the hiring.' So, I thought . . . I'm going to give this guy a call. I did my research on the person doing the hiring, and he was an older gentleman. He didn't have a cellphone, he didn't email, he didn't text, so I knew I had to do it the old-fashioned way. I had to call him. So, every Thursday morning at 9 a.m., I'm going to call this man, and I'm going to try to get a job.

"I called him, introduced myself, and I told myself. I'm going to spend one minute on the phone with him. Just one; I didn't want to waste his time, and I didn't want to be a bother. So, one minute went by, and I introduced myself, told him who I was, told him what I wanted, hung up the phone. Next Thursday, I called again. Fourth Thursday, he said, 'Hello Blake.' He didn't even ask who it was. He knew I was calling. I was being persistent.

"Did the guy hire me? No, but what he did was, he recommended me to the Director of College Scouting with the Houston Oilers, who did hire me. He said, 'this guy's going to work for you. I'm going to tell you right now, he calls me once a week, he really is passionate about what he does.' Persistent people get the jobs, OK?"

Which GM candidates get hired?

In the summer of 2016, I thought it would be interesting to look at the general managers hired in the previous three years. Where did they come from? What did they have in common? What did NFL teams seem to be looking for in the best candidates?

To answer these questions, I looked at the 10 GMs hired from 2014-16. The 10: Ray Farmer (Browns) and Jason Licht (Bucs) in 2014; Mike Maccagnan (Jets), Scot McCloughan (Redskins) and Ryan Pace (Bears) in 2015; and Sashi Brown (Browns), Chris Grier (Dolphins), Bob Quinn (Lions), Jon Robinson (Titans) and Howie Roseman (Eagles) in 2016. Here's what I came up with:

Finished at 50: The oldest GM hired over those three years was Maccagnan at 47, and his hiring came with a bit of an asterisk because his relationship to the man conducting the Jets' search (former Texans and Redskins GM Charley Casserly) was central to his selection. Second-oldest was Grier, and like Maccagnan, he was a bit of an outlier because the real iron in Miami's front office, according to people I've spoken to, belonged to Mike Tannenbaum, the team's Executive Vice President of Football Operations. Toss out those two, and the average age of the last six GMs hired is 40. In fact, all four GMs hired in '16 (except Grier) were 40.

Patriot-ic: Four of the 10 on the list had experience at New England on their respective resumes. Two others, Farmer and Pace, had the Belichick "scent" as Farmer worked under ex-Pats executive Scott Pioli during his time in Kansas City, and Pace was schooled in the Parcells way in New Orleans by head coach Sean Payton. The other four are outliers for different reasons. Brown and Roseman both earned the trust of ownership and worked their way into the GM position from within, while Maccagnan benefited from his time with Casserly. McCloughan had a different, though substantial, pedigree from his status as a Ron Wolf protege.

Some experience necessary: Though all 10 could be considered experienced in league circles, none could have been considered an old hand, per se. Only four (Grier, Licht, Maccagnan and McCloughan) had more than two decades in NFL front offices when they were hired. On the other end of the spectrum, the Browns hired not one, but two, GMs who had 14 years or less in pro football management. Farmer and Brown combined for 26 years' experience when each was hired. That's just two more years than Maccagnan and McCloughan each had (24) when they were hired.

Pedigree matters. Brown is a Harvard Law grad, while the Eagles' Roseman has a Fordham law degree. Robinson initially attended the Air Force Academy; Farmer went to Duke; Grier went to Massachusetts; and Maccagnan went to a highly respected Northeast liberal arts school, Trinity College. Though Licht didn't attend an Ivy League school, he was a pre-med student at Nebraska Wesleyan.

One chance: The days of Ron Wolf struggling in Tampa Bay but drawing on that experience to succeed in Green Bay are probably over, with McCloughan and Roseman the only two hires from 2014-16 with previous GM experience (Roseman essentially returned to the job from a brief in-house hiatus).

Director of Player Personnel? No: No longer does a GM have to hold the title of DPP, the traditional last step before GM. Neither of Cleveland's GM hires, Brown or Farmer, ever made the final call on personnel (though Farmer was assistant GM when he was hired). In addition, Grier and Maccagnan went directly from Director of College Scouting to the GM role.

Playing the media's game

In the days before Inside the League in the early 2000s, I was able to befriend an NFL GM, and we spoke occasionally. He was amazingly forthright and always spoke openly, which I appreciated. At the time (as now), I was thoroughly interested in how information flowed through the league. Why would an NFL scout or administrator risk his highly coveted, hard-to-replace job to tell a beat writer who the team liked in the middle rounds, or even in the early rounds? The GM was succinct.

"I spent some time in the media doing broadcast work between jobs, and I saw that media-friendly GMs and scouting directors always got friendly treatment in return," he said. "It's a quid pro quo relationship. If you give a reporter good inside scoop, he'll take care of you when times are tough."

He added that, most of the time, information that's coming from the bigger media personalities and better-known "draft gurus" was coming from director types, not road scouts. Directors were the ones who benefited from media exposure and the ones who regularly dealt with beat writers.

In succeeding years, it was fascinating to watch him live this out. This GM became one of the most media-friendly, if not *the most* media-friendly, NFL officials in the game. I knew a writer who tells a story about being on the golf course when the GM's team signed its first-rounder, and he got a ring on his cellphone. It was the GM, and while the writer stood on the 15th hole, the GM spelled out in detail the terms of the contract while my friend scribbled madly on his score card. This was an unsolicited call, mind you. That's a GM who's eager to stay on writers' good sides.

I got a different dose of reality when I was chatting with a longtime member of the scouting community who was between jobs. During our conversation, he mentioned an active NFL head coach and how much he respected his work ethic and smarts before his voice trailed off. I could tell there were things he'd left unsaid, so I asked him what he didn't like about the coach.

"He thinks about his career first," he said. "He's always talking to the media. That's why he has his job now, why he got a head coaching position. He'd been feeding the media for years, and it paid off."

I could tell you dozens of stories in this vein, from how agents control information release to how NFL officials have benefited from cozy relationships with people on the representation or media side.

On becoming a scouting assistant

Each spring, I work with several ITL clients who are trying to break into the league as scouting assistants and interns. After listening to the progress they're making and the obstacles they're seeing, I've come to several realizations about the process and what teams are seeking. Here are a few thoughts.

- **Every team is different:** I need to start with this disclaimer. Some teams are looking for young people to do things around the office, gather information, file things, take calls, make copies, and the kind of grunt work that all interns do everywhere, but with a football spin to it. On the other hand, some teams' scouting assistants spend a lot of time picking up dry cleaning, making airport runs or running other errands that have no football peg whatsoever. In fact, if you listed their day-to-day chores, you might not even know they worked for NFL teams. One of my best scouting assistant candidates interviewed with a team that told him, "You need to go straight to area scout." That team wasn't prepared for his level of preparation and professionalism, and in fact, that's why he didn't get hired.

- **If you're over 27, forget about scouting:** Several years ago, I had a long exchange with a good friend who aspires to work for an NFL team. He'd spent a lot of time and money getting as qualified to be an NFL scout as possible, but he was well into his 30s. I felt I had to break it to him that scouting assistants don't get hired when they leave their 20s. I certainly don't say this to crush your spirits if you're 30-plus, but teams are looking for young, cheap people they can mold. Unless you're coming out of a lengthy playing career for a team, they're not going to invest in you if you're on the wrong side of 30.

- **It's not always about scouting:** Teams don't even want you to think of yourself as a scout when you enter the building. In fact, I think most teams want their interns and scouting assistants to be blank slates: completely formless and willing to do anything. In many cases, football is something scouting assistants almost do in their free time. If you've already begun to develop a scouting eye, this could be a detriment, because most teams want to teach you and monitor your progress rather than having to unwind bad habits you might have developed. This is why I'm starting to believe earning accreditations and taking scouting-related classes is a bad idea. The NFL just isn't ready for this yet. When teams have thousands of people to choose from, they just want cheap labor. They don't want quasi-professionals. This is an important point, and this is why the best route to the NFL still goes through college recruiting and personnel offices.

- **Don't apply online to sports job services:** A few services have developed that aggregate sports jobs online. This is not how scouting assistants are hired. In fact, if your best shot at getting a scouting job is applying through some similar link, you should buy a lottery ticket the same day you send in your resume because the odds of success are the same.

- **Forget about Draft Twitter:** If you think that you can pad your credentials for an NFL job by becoming a Twitter scout, think again. Yes, Daniel Jeremiah rode his Twitter account to a place on the NFL Network, and several other ex-NFL scouts have had varying levels of success with Twitter, but the key is they had *already* been in the league. No NFL team is reading Twitter takes and saying, "We gotta have that guy."

As always, I don't dispense these thoughts to destroy peoples' dreams, and God knows there are exceptions to all of these rules. Still, having heard stories and seen hiring in action, these conclusions were inescapable. I hope they help.

A note about volunteering

One thing I harp on with people seeking to climb the football business ladder is that, one time or another, you'll have to work for free. In fact, in most cases, you'll have to work not only for free, but probably at some cost.

How many times have I worked for free? My gosh, it's countless. I've driven all over Texas to cover a football clinic or work a combine, all on my own dime; spent $300-plus (a lot for me at the time) on a phone bill generated by my (volunteer) work on my first-ever all-star game (plus burned a week of vacation to help run the game); gotten stiffed on speaking engagements; and flown to New Orleans to interview for a job that provided only a stipend had I gotten it (I didn't). These are but a few instances, and I'm sure if I had more time I could fill this book with them.

But here's the point: all of these experiences gave me currency with people. They helped me speak with some level of expertise on some pretty nuanced football-related subjects. They gave me the mentors I've used to help me advance in the business and build my service. There's no way I could ever have done it if not for these sometimes-awkward times in my professional life.

More insights and advice on breaking into the business

"I got the (Saints) internship through a family friend. My father was real good friends with (Hall of Fame former Saints linebacker) Rickey Jackson, and . . . I had just graduated from college, and he asked my dad, 'what's Barrett doing?' And he said, 'he's working, looking for a job,' and (Jackson) said, 'well, since he's doing that, I'm going to attempt to get him an internship.' After that, I went to interview, and fortunately got the internship and it just grew from there. I was the kid who was always around, whether it was 6 o'clock in the morning or 2 o'clock in the morning. Whenever they needed me, I was there.

"I became a scout after . . . we had all the changeover between (former head coach Mike) Ditka and (then-Saints GM) Randy Mueller at the time. The acting general manager, interim general manager Charles Bailey, he looked in-house for some help on the football side to watch tape. He knew I was a guy who played football, who had football in my blood, and he said, 'Well, just watch this tape,' and I want to say it was the defensive lineman from Florida State, Corey Simon. He said, 'Barrett, watch this tape and tell me what you think of it.' I was watching tape, and I was saying, 'he's explosive, he's powerful, he can run, he can do XYZ.' I was saying things in crude elementary terms because I didn't have the terminology down, but he saw that I could evaluate guys, you know, I don't want to say instantly, but I had an eye for that.

"Then . . . after I did my duties with the media relations department, because that was what my internship was, I would go there after hours and help out. After Randy Mueller came in, everyone that was in place, he just left them in place because of the time constraints, because he came on either right before or right after the Senior Bowl of 2000, so with that said, I just did whatever they needed.

"I used to joke with our football assistant that I was 'the special man.' Whether that was driving players to medical, to physicals, picking players up at the airport, babysitting them, getting cell phones for the coaches, whatever they needed, I did it. So then, by me not being afraid of work, they said, well, we have a position open, and he's earned a shot at it, and I was given the job of West Coast scout for the 2001 season. I did that for two years, then I transitioned to combine scout, which goes to colleges in a specific area and evaluates guys going from junior to a rising senior." – **Barrett Wiley, former Saints area scout**

"I was coaching in the CFL (Canadian Football League) and there were issues with the ownership at the time, with them bouncing checks to name a few things. I got to know an individual that worked with Kansas City who used to come to Canada and scout. We struck up a conversation about scouting, and they happened to have an opening. It took a little doing, by having people call on my behalf to the individual that was doing the hiring in the personnel department. As you would have guessed, it isn't always *what* you know, but *who* you know. Once I got in, my boss told me that it was now my job to stay in, and that was (about two decades) ago." – **Mike Murphy, former NFL scout (Chiefs, Seahawks, Cowboys, Dolphins, Giants)**

"If I met a young person who wanted to be a scout I would advise them to contact their local NFL team and volunteer to work in their personnel department. Also, contact local colleges and volunteer to work in their scouting department. Then make friends with everyone involved in the organization, because you never know who is going to advance into a position where they can make hiring decisions." – **Joe Bommarito, former Jets area scout**

"Well, as it came about, I was finished playing ball, so I'd come back (to Kingsville, Texas had gone to college) and wanted to get my degree and wanted to get into coaching. So I was back, and went to New Orleans to visit a buddy of mine. They had hired a new general manager at the time, and it was Randy Mueller, and I knew Randy very, very well. He was one of the reasons, as a player, that I went to Seattle, from Canada. I just so happened to stop by the office, and didn't get to see him but left my resume. We stayed in touch and what have you, and it got down to the last week, and they were ready to go, and he called me up and said, 'Hey, are you really serious about doing this?' I said, 'Yeah, I really am. I like to learn.' And I had kinda told him while I was playing ball that I wouldn't mind getting in this business. I went out and interviewed, and he gave me the job. It was a good deal. I was fortunate with Randy. Randy kinda trusted me, and I really trusted him. He's the type of guy (who) believed in what guys around him said. He really took to heart what guys around him said. He made that transition for me (from player to scout) very easy." -- **James Jefferson, former Seahawks safety and Saints area scout**

"John Ralston . . . was the head football coach of the Denver Broncos (from 1972-76). Well, I was in high school coaching and I wrote him a letter . . . because I wanted to get into something besides high school coaching. I wrote him a letter, and he visited with me. I went down to his office, and we talked about it, and he was a great guy, great motivating coach and all that stuff. But he said, 'Well, we don't have interns and graduate assistants like you have on the college level,' so he kind of pooh-

poohed it. But I still wrote (a letter to the Washington Redskins), because I remember (reading in a) Sports Illustrated article, ('70s Redskins head coach) George (Allen) talking about (having an interest in hiring high school coaches as scouts).

"So, I wrote the letter, and one of the stipulations of becoming an intern was my dad had to co-sign a letter of credit for me, because (Allen) didn't want us to go there without any financial backing. . . What's really interesting about the whole thing is that this was 1976, and I was the head football coach (at a Colorado high school), assistant basketball coach and I taught history and earth science. I was making $15,000 a year doing all those things. I went to the NFL for nothing, with a $10,000 line of credit, but they would give me $600 to go out on the road, so I actually ended up making more money working for nothing than I did as a high school coach, which tells you something about high school and public education and that sort of thing." – **Miller McCalmon, former Bills and Oilers assistant coach and former Redskins, Lions and Texans scout**

"(Bears Director of College Scouting Mark) Sadowski wants to be an NFL coach. So, once a month, he prints out 32 resumes and sends one to every NFL team but gets no responses. After a while, he calls Omar Khan, a friend from Tulane who now is with the Saints. 'If I give you a handful of my resumes, would you mind putting one in the head coach's mailbox every week?' he says. Khan initially is hesitant, but he agrees, placing one of Sadowski's resumes in Mike Ditka's mailbox every Friday for a couple of months. Finally, Sadowski gets a call from Saints pro personnel director Chet Franklin. He asks if Sadowski is interested in a pro scouting job. Sadowski tells him no. He wants to be a coach. After some back and forth, Sadowski agrees to an interview. Franklin calls him for a second interview. At this interview, he meets Ditka. After he shakes his hand, Sadowski marvels at how big it is. Ditka: 'You're the one who keeps sending me resumes.' Sadowski: 'I'm sorry, coach, I apologize.' Ditka: 'Oh no, I like that. Hey Chet, I like this kid. He's from Chicago. Hire him.' " – **Dan Pompei of The Athletic, "Bears' scouting director Mark Sadowski lives a life straight out of the movies," April 2, 2020**

"Quick advice is, you better have thick skin, and you better look up the word 'sacrifice,' because if you are going to be in this business, you are going to have to sacrifice a lot. Be patient. Everybody says they want to be the GM by 30. You have to be patient and embrace the grind of it. You might make ($17,000) for five years while all of your other buddies are making $70-80,000 going to happy hour three times a week. Well, you might get to go once a month or you only get one month a year to do stuff. The young group needs to embrace the whole 'grind' aspect of it and know that they have to be 100 percent patient and that it is not going to be a quick-and-easy process. You are going to sacrifice everything. Family. Friends. Girlfriends. Where you live. Everything." – **Scott Aligo, Director of Player Personnel at Michigan State and former Browns area scout**

"No. 1, research. No. 2, persistence. No. 3, don't be afraid to think outside the box to develop a relationship with the person who makes the hiring decisions. No. 4, get lucky. And all of this applies across the spectrum. If you were going in for an interview with Apple, you would want to know everything about Jim Smith (the boss). . . You (may not) have the best GPA and you (may not) have that big of an interest in technology on your resume. That doesn't matter. If you get in front of Jim and you have the charisma, the personality, and you know how to interact with people on a mature level and he's looking to hire somebody, he's not going to forget that. It's not about the degree, it's not about the GPA, it's how you fit in with the team that matters." – **Matt Boockmeier, Edmonton Eskimos area scout and former Packers and Saints area scout**

"It's a very cutthroat business. It's a small business, and it's hard to get in because a lot of people want to do it and there are not a lot of jobs. It's a very limited field. But one thing that is important is to immerse yourself in football in any way that you can. If you're a kid in college and you've never played before, work the equipment or video for your team. A lot of guys make their first steps in the game that way. Show that you are working. It's not just putting your foot in the door, it's someone being able to say that you work hard. If you work in video or you are a coach's assistant of some kind, from that, just absorb everything around you. Maybe a scout comes into your school and you are helping with the video, introduce yourself. He may pick your brain. Find a way to make a connection with someone in the game but also show that you can bring that work ethic or that awareness. If you are around athletes, pick up on how does that guy treat other people or what is he like personally away from the cameras, away from the spotlight. Also, watch as much film as you can. If you have the ability to get your hands on a coach's tape, write reports. Evaluate positions you don't necessarily understand; show progress and show growth that way. I played linebacker in college and I played offensive line in high school, so those things came more naturally to me than wide receiver and DB. So, I had to force myself to watch DB tape and pick up on nuances. Put yourself out there. Volunteer if you have to. Do those little things to show you are committed. Also, watch as much football as you possibly can. You aren't out of your realm because you have basic knowledge on what to pick up on." – **Marcus Hendrickson, Director of Player Personnel at Minnesota and former Dolphins and Browns area scout**

"Make sure you have some background in football. Maybe you were a player or worked with some of the colleges. Scouting is evolving. With analytics, you don't necessarily have to take the traditional route of starting in football. With analytics, some guys have made their way up through the charting process into a building. It is evolving that way, but the rule of thumb is you have a background in football. Your network is pivotal when you are trying to break in. Knowing someone who can get your resume from someone else to (speak) on your behalf. All of these teams get thousands of emails every year, and I don't know if they look at them all, but most of the time it's knowing someone who can put your name in front of someone who can look at your resume and give you an interview." – **Redskins (and former Browns) area scout Harrison Ritcher**

"The most important thing is to be involved. Find a way to be involved. Your resume should show you have a passion for football, whether it's coaching high school football or helping out at the college level or finding a way to work for an arena team or whatever it may be. The door is not always open as far as NFL scouting jobs go, but every single person who works at that level did something before that. If you can get involved in some way, then that's going to go a long way as far as getting your foot in the door somewhere else. For me, I didn't play college football. I got my foot in the door in the weight room. From there, I worked at football operations and recruiting at a big college, and then I met people and got a chance to go to the NFL at an entry-level job. I think you just have to find a way to get involved and stay involved. It speaks to the person's passion if you see them being involved with it." – **Matt Lindsey, General Manager at Ole Miss and former Philadelphia Eagles college scouting coordinator**

"Seek out contacts and follow up with them. If you do that, the main thing to do is to not quit or get discouraged when you are told no. In my case, I only had one team call back out of the 32 I sent my resume, and I wound up being one guy out of seven auditioning for an intern position. If I would have listened to all of those letters that said 'no, no, no,' I would have just quit." – **Morocco Brown, Colts Director of College Scouting; he has also served on the scouting staffs of the Bears, Redskins and Browns**

"A scout's job is to write a report and explain that player to the GM, head coach and other assistants, and have all the information to back it up, along with the film. I don't think it will ever happen, but I would like to see former players hired as scouts. They just have to be trained like I was. I think the benefits (would) be long-lasting because former players have been in the trenches and our minds think much differently than a scout who was hired because his grandfather or uncle is the GM/HC of the team." – **Bruce Plummer, a former defensive back for five NFL teams and a former Falcons area scout**

"When I hire scouts or assemble a staff, I want people that can check their ego at the door. It's not about getting *your* guys drafted. It's about us drafting the *right guys*. I despise people who think it's their job to sell the players in their area. I want those guys who can find and identify exactly our prioritized characteristics, that *we* want as an organization. Some people can look at film all day, but can't identify the traits that are important. The second-most important thing is I want *opinions*. I don't want 'yes' men. I want you to identify the characteristics that we define and speak on them with detail. I actually think scouts get better with perspective and experience. I wanted older, experienced scouts who were not afraid to express their opinions so we could build consensus. Younger, information-gathering scouts can become this, but it's gonna take time and, as they say, education is expensive." – **Randy Mueller, former NFL executive with the Seahawks, Saints, Dolphins and Chargers**

CHAPTER 4
Losing the job

In March 2020, during the height of the coronavirus outbreak, several of my agent clients began contacting me, asking me what to do as pro days had been canceled. I saw only one possibility: round up as many former NFL scouts as I could find and attempt to plug them into agent-organized pro days across the country. My hope was that their presence would lend these workouts credibility in the absence of alternatives. So, agents stepped forward, found locations and engaged video services. I matched them up with ex-NFL evaluators in their local markets.

It was an incredible three weeks. We held workouts at gyms, colleges, on tracks at high schools, everywhere. One agent asked me to find a scout who would time his client running down a hallway. I helped link scouts and agents who were in different states. Sometimes, my scouts would be paid nearly $1,000 to spend an hour working out one player. One day in Dallas, two coaches actually got into a fistfight mid-workout. It was mass hysteria.

Anyway, I got a lot of pushback from friend and foe alike on our workouts, but we pressed forward. To our pleasant surprise, several teams reached out to ask us for our numbers, and several scouts reached out to our pro day "proctors" to ask them about the workouts. In other words, the 13 ex-scouts we used were professional, reliable, unassailable. "If we get it from the (former) scouts, then we are going to put the info in our system," a scout with one team told me. "We are a little cautious of putting testing numbers received from agents in, even if they note who tested the player."

If all of these scouts were seasoned and trustworthy, why weren't they still working for NFL teams? Here's what I think.

Scouting departments are the first ones cut for budgetary reasons: I don't know why this is. I remember having this discussion with an agent a few years back, and we talked about how much money Fortune 500 companies plow into their budgets for research and development. For whatever reason, NFL teams (which are virtually 32 Fortune 500 companies) are exactly the opposite. When the bean counters come, they most often come for the scouting departments.

Scouts are seen as dispensable: I remember one time at the all-star game I serve, the College Gridiron Showcase, there was a sponsor whose service could completely scan a prospect's social media and find all the problems. I was talking later to a scout about it, and he said, "Why would we pay for something like that? We have dozens of scouting assistants and interns around that have nothing to do." As of this writing, the Titans are the only team that posts scouting openings on the web, and I've always wondered how many thousands of applications they get for those positions. When there are so, so many people lining up for a job, I guess it's easy to be pretty fickle about the guys you have.

There's no metric for scout evaluation: I've hunted high and low to find a team that grades its scouts. In almost 20 years running a football consulting service, I've never found one. I get it. The draft picks that make a roster are a function of so many things that it's hard to attribute it solely to the scout in their area.

What's more, there is a regional bias in play. The scouts assigned to the Southeast are going to have more players on pro rosters than their counterparts in the Northwest, every year.

Because there's no metric, it's all about connections: One year I was considering starting a training service for scouts, so I called a friend who was at the director level with a team. I asked him, "When you're looking to hire a scouting assistant, what do you look for?" His reply: "You got somebody?" I'd say, more often than not, that's how scouts are hired, even today.

The spoils system: This is a corollary to the "old boy" element. When a new GM comes in, everyone understands he's going to surround himself with people he trusts, just as a head coach does with his staff. Because scouts are generally on two-year deals, usually making around $100,000 per year, there's never a lot of controversy when the ax falls on a scout, even if he's been with the team for years. Everyone just kind of shrugs and understands.

If you aren't on the GM track, you're on shaky ground: I think many GMs seek out the scouts who have the eye for talent as well as the confidence, the look, the aura of a future star, and they keep you around. Simply being a good evaluator, paying your dues, keeping your head down and getting your work done is not good enough if you're not a little sexy.

Even good scouts are mostly anonymous: Unless you're an absolute NFL maniac, I bet you can't name an area scout on any NFL team without Google. On the other hand, it's not hard to name the offensive and defensive coordinators on most teams. There are no headlines when a team fires its Director of College Scouting, and no one ever asks for the autograph of the team's midlands area scout. Therefore, the GM can fire scouts he doesn't like and not have to worry about social media blowback or heat from the owner.

Examining the changes

In the summer of 2018, we took a look at the post-draft staffing changes, looking for hiring trends by comparing them to what had happened after the 2017 draft. With new full-time GMs in New York, Charlotte, Cleveland, Houston and Green Bay, it was expected that 2018 would offer an incredibly busy offseason. However, while there were 170 moves up, down or out after the '17 draft, we tracked only 89 moves in the same time frame, the month after the '18 draft.

At any rate, here are a few observations.

- For a while, it looked like colleges would become the logical landing spot for ex-scouts, but we only tracked two such hires (Tampa Bay's Pat Perles to Kansas as an analyst and Atlanta's Kevin Simon to Tennessee in a player development role) that offseason. Why? A new rule allowing a 10th coach on the field in college football is credited with pulling money away from the personnel side and into the coaching side.

- We counted 30 members of scouting and personnel who got let go between the end of the '16 season and start of the '17 season. Of that 30, only 10 made it back into the scouting profession before May 2018. What's more, only eight of them were back in the NFL (former Chiefs exec Will Lewis and ex-Titans scout Tim Ruskell were hired as GMs in the now-defunct Alliance of American Football).

- Area scouts seemed as disposable as ever, and maybe more so. Nine area scouts were let go after the '17 draft. Only one — former Bills scout Shawn Heinlen, who was hired by the Eagles — was back in the league before June 2018.

- The reason seemed to be that teams elevated their own people. We counted 11 area scouts hired that spring (though they have various specific titles), and of the 11, five — about half — were in-house hires as either promotions or reassignments.

- Staying in-house was actually part of a larger trend. Sixty people got hired to new jobs that spring. Of those 60, 24 didn't have to change addresses. Again, almost half.

- At the same time that it's hard to get a second job in scouting, loyalty isn't always valued, either. Of the 23 scouts and executives who were dumped that offseason, eight had never worked for another team.

- Looking over the five years heading into 2018, about 20 scouts got fired every year and didn't return. They varied in experience, time with team and success of the team firing them. With about 250 jobs across the league in scouting and evaluation, that's around 10 percent.

- At the end of the day, the only things to know for sure are that it's a volatile business; loyalty and personal relationships are critical. Once you get in, work as hard as you can not to get out.

More insights on surviving (and not surviving)

"Regions are (a) difficult (way) to say (that) one scout is better than another because the quality of players are different from each region. Some conferences are known for their offensive linemen, while others are known for their skill positions. Traditionally, one of your better scouts is placed in the Southeast, but that does not mean he is the best scout. Scouts are looked at in different ways; how they fit in with other scouts, how he does gathering information, (how he) presents that information, and does he get his work done in a timely manner? Some places are known for having their scouts more as information-gatherers than evaluators, and place a high importance on the information-gathering. Others are known to lean on their scouts as evaluators, not just information-gatherers. This is not an exact science; otherwise scouts would not be needed. You want to get more right than you get wrong, or you won't be in the NFL long. I don't know any team that has a set of guidelines to evaluate scouts. You do have some individuals who are IE's (Instant Evaluators) and look at where players are drafted compared to a scout's grade. The issue with being an IE is that your team or another may have made a mistake on a player but may not know for three years. The best way I know to evaluate a scout is the same as a player. Give them three years. Players will wash out somewhere around the three-year mark. Scouts are the same way (to see if they are any good). There typically will be a good year, a down year, and hopefully by the third year they have evened out and settled into their role." -- **Mike Murphy, former area scout, Seahawks, Chiefs, Dolphins & Giants**

"We get usually two years, and I came back and did two more years, and then after that, everybody here knows, kind of all heck broke loose at the Rams, right? We had a terrible season, (and) Coach (Jeff) Fisher gets fired. You've got to understand, at some point, when you're hired to scout, (or) whatever you do, you might have to fall on the sword, right? . . . (GM) Les (Snead) was in trouble, OK? A couple of us had to fall on the sword, and that's not what you want. It hurts. It stinks, not fun, but at the end of the day, I got a chance to do what I wanted, and I will always be thankful for Les, and (Senior Personnel Adviser) Taylor (Morton) for bringing me into that building. I don't like the way it ended, (but) you don't have to like it, and I had to figure out how to bounce back some way, one way or the other. But that's kind of my story. It's kind of unique how it happened." -- **Danton Barto, former area scout, Rams**

"I was with the Browns for seven years, and went through four different general managers. And each time a new general manager came on, it was like, you're on a four-month job interview. I remember one year, (new Browns GM) Phil Savage was at the East-West game in California, and we changed our whole grading scale there. He said, 'Hey, look guys, I'm going to do it this way -- we're going to change the grading scale. Here it is. Go for it.' So, we had to go back in and regrade all of our guys. As it ended up, Phil actually signed me to a three-year contract, because he liked the work I did. So then Phil, he's under the gun for reasons out of his control, because we had finished 10-6 and just missed the playoffs. We had drafted six Pro Bowlers, but things didn't work out. So, then we went through three straight years of different general managers, different head coaches, and each year, there's three months where you're working for a new guy, with a new rating system, and you're trying to find your way. Finally, it ended up, I wasn't renewed one year by one guy . . . And I was an easy guy to get out because everybody else had contracts (with time left). So, I was let out of that job." – **Bob Morris, former area scout, 49ers and Browns**

"I believe some of the volatility can be attributed to owners getting less and less patient with keeping GMs and coaches in place if they are not producing within a three-year span and them staying consistent. They are getting more and more pressure from the fans to make changes as well (if) the team is not doing well. It used to be GMs would get a chance to at least hire two coaches, sometimes three, before the owners would start looking at them for replacement. Now it's down to two and sometimes only one chance to hire a head coach. Bottom line, owners want results more quickly than they did in the past. Then the thing about GMs is you only get one shot at it. You can probably count on one hand how many two-time GMs there are in the league." – **Cedric Saunders, former Senior Vice President of Football Operations with the Lions, now an agent with Goal Line Football**

CHAPTER 5
Doing the Job

My friend Mike Murphy has been a scout for several NFL teams. He comes from good bloodlines as his father, Cal, was a longtime CFL coach and scout. I asked him to give me a scout's full-day schedule.

"You set your schedule in camp before you leave, and for the most part, you are gone 10 days to two weeks at a time. This can get drawn out but here goes. If you are a morning person and like to work out, this is the best time to do it, so you are usually up around 5-5:30 a.m. to get an hour in, followed by eating breakfast and be at your school somewhere around 7-8 a.m. depending on what time the school allows you in. You sit in a dark room by yourself or with other scouts and grind out the game tape. The game tape is not what you see on TV. There is no sound, and it is a sideline and end-zone view, and you watch a minimum of three games plus special teams. The biggest issue is to stay focused when it is quiet and you are in a dark room. At some point during the day, the pro liaison will come and talk to you regarding the players. He will either get into an in-depth conversation on players, or he will be vague. That will depend on the policy of the program set by the head coach.

"If you have watched the tape and spoken with the pro liaison, the next thing is (to) speak with the athletic trainer, strength coach and academic adviser. If you can get to a position coach, coordinator or head coach, talk to them, too. All of these interviews help you build a bio/background on an individual player. This background can, and will, have a big bearing on the individual's draft status. You want to dig and see if the individual can learn. And if he struggles, is it terminal, or is there a certain way he learns, and can he retain the information given to him? This will help also when you talk to your coaches about an individual player letting them know that there might be some issues with the player's ability to learn. What we find are a lot of players that have reading comprehension issues. This causes a problem because of the volume of information given to players each and every day during training camp and the installation of an offense or defense.

"After you finish with your interviews, you head out to practice to get body types and watch the players move around. The body typing is helpful in many ways to see growth potential, for example. Are they a small-boned individual or big-boned? Large-boned players are usually naturally big and not self-made, allowing them to put on more weight, as opposed to a small-boned individual who is self-made, not naturally big, and who is susceptible to injury. Is a lineman narrow-hipped, knock-kneed, high-cut (long legs)? This will affect his ability to create power or anchor and play with good consistent leverage.

"Once you have gotten all your information and watched practice, you head to the car to drive to your next town. It could be a hop, skip and a jump down the road or a four- to five-hour drive, sometimes more. Most times, you are done with practice between 4-5 in the afternoon. Once you get to your next destination, you may have grabbed dinner on the road, or you get dinner and start typing your reports. In any event, you do not start typing reports until after dinner (time frame). I have been up until 1 a.m. typing reports, but most evenings will (end) somewhere around 11p.m., and you are up and back at it all over again the next day.

"The job has its perks, and where else do they pay you to watch football? The thing is, it isn't as glamorous as people think, and it is a grind. Most times, come November, there are a bunch of grumpy scouts, and that will affect how you view a player. You do find yourself coming out of camp being more lenient, but come November, you become much less lenient."

Doing the job: Take 2

My friend Ken Moll has seen it all in his time as a college football coach as well as a scout with the Cleveland Browns, Jacksonville Jaguars and the CFL Winnipeg Blue Bombers. I asked Ken to take me through a week on the road as an area scout.

"If you're a football fan, I'm sure it sounds glamorous to travel to schools like Notre Dame, Ohio State, Florida State and Alabama to evaluate players. OK, maybe it *is* a *little* glamorous.

"On the other hand, try checking in and out of four hotels in five nights while traveling through West Virginia. That junket might involve a Morgantown-to-Glenville-State stretch (both places former Arizona and Michigan head coach Rich Rodriguez has coached), possibly checking out a free agent at Concord College or Fairmont State after (or before) a stop in Huntington. From there, it's a several-hour trip to Blacksburg, Va., to attend a Saturday afternoon Virginia Tech game.

"The next morning is Sunday. Time to get some sleep? Not quite. I need to catch up on my player reports – which I work on two-three hours a night during the week – then it's usually laundry day and getting my travel expenses together while settling in to watch *my* team play on Sunday afternoon.

"Come Monday, I start my day usually 7:15 a.m.-ish (no later than 8) with a trip to the school's film room. At some point, I may thank heavens that we live in the digital age; the old-timers tell stories of having to splice 16 mm film together when it broke after running plays back numerous times.

"After 3-4 game tapes (on each side of the ball) and several cups of coffee, it's time to visit with the trainer, strength coach and pro liaison. These information-gathering meetings may take place in consecutive stints, but they're most likely chopped up throughout the day (as you're on their time schedule). It takes time to decipher which information is reliable and which isn't. It's a wonder why some within an organization wouldn't be totally forthright when discussing one of their own, but I digress. Sometimes it's tricky deciding which information will be part of your official report. This is why experience is extremely important when covering a territory, as relationships built over time tend to produce the most reliable information. That's important when you're evaluating not only their game tape, but their injuries, character, weight room numbers and work ethic.

"Along the way, you might get an hour to grab lunch before practice. Sometimes, your lunchtime occurs when you have to vacate the film room for a team's positional meetings before practice.

"Practice is approximately two-plus hours (depending on the day of the week) and a great time for up-close access to players you have scrutinized on tape most of the day. You always make note of body types, i.e., high-cut, short arms, soft body, etc., while getting a feel for work ethic and how a player reacts to the ups and downs of competing in practice. You can really see how quickly a quarterback releases the ball, the closing burst of a cornerback or the 'get-off' burst of a defensive end when evaluating a live practice. You also get to see how a player reacts to coaches' criticism as well as how he relates to his teammates (is he a leader?).

"There are other subtleties you can pick up. How does he treat the student trainer when he needs to have his ankle taped during the middle of practice? How does he relate to the assistant equipment manager that has to fix his face mask after a grueling hit in a live goal-line drill?

"Most scouts leave the practice field at the beginning of the 'team' period; often the college coaches prefer it that way as they are installing game plans, trick plays, etc. and the pace may be a little slower.

"If you're lucky, travel to your next destination is less than an hour, but often it's much more than that. Your routine becomes checking into the hotel, getting some grub, then maybe catching some relaxation time. After that, what do you think you do with all those notes and information gathered during the day? You got it. You get on the computer and usually bang out at least a couple of hours of reports before you get some shut-eye. The next morning, sometime before daybreak, you get ready to do it all over again.

"If this sound glamorous, you're 'approved' to proceed with your dreams of becoming an NFL scout. And maybe a little crazy."

Scouting an all-star game

I also asked Ken for his thoughts on all-star games and how he approached them. The following passage includes Ken's thoughts on the topic.

"My thoughts on all-star games are mixed. I have attended the week of practices for almost 40 all-star game and evaluated more than 500 players during that time.

"Depending on how the director structures the evaluation process, scouts may be exposed to players they haven't seen prior to that week. Some personnel departments will have each scout concentrate on players from his assigned region. I much preferred to evaluate a position, as was the case most of the time for me. My favorite way to do it was to follow an entire group the week of padded practices (Monday through Wednesday), then attend the game (which didn't happen often; most scouts depart before the game is played). By the time I had broken down the practice and game tapes, I had a great perspective on how a player fit alongside like-caliber athletes at the same position. I really enjoyed all-star practices as you can see specific drills (individual, one on one, inside-outside and team periods) with all of the highest-level players in one spot.

"The best thing about these games is that you get great exposure to your assigned group, on and off the field. If you know what the coaching staff is trying to get out of a player (technique, scheme, etc.), it can be very helpful in knowing what you've seen and how you grade a player at the end of the week. Also, having access to each player in an interview setting is very helpful in getting to know what makes a player tick.

"All-star game weeks are part of the puzzle for every scout, personnel director, coaching staff and GM. That being said, don't let the old bromide that 'you can't lose ground on your draft status in an all-star game' fool you. Everything a player does or doesn't do in any game, practice, interview, workout or combine matters. It does affect his draft status. Now, there's a difference between 'graded players' and 'players that have grades.' What I mean by that is, some collegiate players have done so much for such an extended period of time that their grade is pretty much set in stone, regardless of what they might do in an all-star game. On the other hand, many players 'have grades,' but there is some uncertainty within an organization on how solid that grade is.

"I have seen players gain draft status (sometimes, two or even three rounds) after an outstanding all-star week. And, yes, I've seen players lose ground with a poor all-star week. Often the biggest swing (draft status or grade) can come from when a small-college player makes it to a higher level all-star game and really impresses versus tougher competition. Believe me, if you accept an invitation to compete in an all-star game, you better be ready to perform at a high level, as all of that is discussed at some point in the draft process."

The art of the cross-check

I'm going to let Ken explain one more topic: the second look that a scout gives other scouts' work, which is called cross-checking.

"Cross-checking -- reviewing the prospects other area scouts on the team have seen (and liked) to verify their opinions -- is an important part of the overall puzzle. Scouting isn't an exact science, but effective cross-checking can provide for a more secure decision. Of course, it's not easy. Obviously, the travel isn't as familiar, but more importantly, the exposure to the players is limited compared to the previous scout, who had much more time to conduct the evaluation.

"What's more, I learned early in my scouting career that it takes balls to go against the grain and to counter the 'conventional wisdom' on high-profile players. Obviously, every scout sees, reads and hears about most draftable collegiate players, but blocking the "noise" out is extremely important to the evaluation process.

"Another thing that makes cross-checking difficult is that it takes place after a long, hard slog through the meat of the season. I remember one of my first seasons in the league (as a Midwest area scout for Jacksonville), my cross-check area was the West Coast. Hitting 11 colleges in 15 days can be a daunting task, especially after a full schedule of three-and-a-half months of travel through Big Ten country. Come November, going from the Arizona schools to Stanford, Cal, USC, UCLA and Fresno State, then out to New Mexico and New Mexico State, as well as a trip up to the great Northwest (University of Washington, State, Oregon and Oregon State and others) is exhausting. There was also a stop in the state of Utah (where I wasn't able to find a good cup of coffee at the campus at BYU), that really was difficult. No one was more excited about settling in at home for a Thanksgiving meal.

"One other thought on cross-checking. It's amazing how one 'set of eyes' sees a particular player differently from another scout. Often this is due to a player being injured at a particular time during the season, or the marked improvement of a player due to more playing time or a better understanding of the position that enhanced his development. Many people outside the industry tend to develop an opinion of collegiate players based on limited information and exposure, whereas NFL scouts are better-qualified to grade a player. This is because their evaluations are based on their experience and knowledge of specific programs, how a player is coached; and what has been successful in the past."

Dealing with schools

One might think that all schools want to see their players drafted, right? It brings press and prestige to the program and helps a team land the next big recruits. As I said, one would think.

Well, one would be wrong, at least in some cases. We polled several scouts to get their opinions on which schools give them the most problems. Some were diplomatic, some less so. I'll let the scouts do the talking.

Here are five responses we got from different scouts. Auburn was the only school named more than once, and it was named three times.

- "All schools are different. Some (are) certainly 'easier' than others based on a lot of factors. But in the end, it's a long evaluation process, and teams generally get what they need."

- "So many bad ones and so many very good ones. Alabama, Arkansas, Missouri, UCLA, Arizona, Florida, Oregon, Stanford, would be at the top of the lists . . . Worst visits would be K-State, Louisville (and) used to be Texas . . .

(Former Texas head coach) Mack Brown was a really good guy, but you had to work really hard to get information. . . Basically, there are some difficult coaches who make your job difficult."

- "TCU, Georgia Tech and Auburn come to mind. They just restrict viewing practice and when you can visit. (Auburn has) actually gotten better. Georgia Tech is possibly the worst in the South. They only let you watch practice for 12 minutes. (Former head coach Paul Johnson) doesn't care."

- "Most of the colleges out west are pretty good. Sometimes, some of the SEC schools can be difficult. But it's different with different steps. Sometimes you can go to Alabama or Georgia and you're great to deal with, but under a different staff there, (it's) tougher to deal with. Same thing with any other college. . . Obviously, all the big schools have high-end equipment and some of the lower-end schools (Division II, Division III) and some of the traditionally African-American schools sometimes don't have as good equipment. . . ."

- "Auburn, Michigan and Michigan State to name a few. (Auburn head coach Gus Malzahn) is odd, but his assistants are good people."

- "Auburn and Oklahoma State."

"The offseason"

The perception is that after the June mini-camp is over, that's pretty much it for the NFL until players report in late July. However, I didn't know for certain if that was true, so I reached out to several scouts and other friends in executive-level positions.

Most area scouts I spoke to said their teams give them the summer off, for the most part. "I drink beer, go to concerts and (baseball) games," said one scout. "Re-charge and do my fall schedule. I work for a team that values family time."

Another agreed that it's basically off time for the summer. "Post-draft is usually the first chance scouts get to somewhat relax," he said. "To me, the best course of action is to take time and decompress."

Of course, other teams see the summer as catch-up time. "Some teams have their scouts immediately begin watching tape and having all the future draftable players in next year's draft written up by July 1," one scout said. "I've had where I watched tape the entire summer. You're worn out already on tape by time camp begins."

Watching tape is part of the summer activities for several scouts I polled. "I like to watch at least a few games of every prospect I will see in the fall," one scout told me. "If I spread it out correctly, the workload isn't too much, and it helps me get ahead for the fall."

The one thing that seems to be universal during the summer, at least for area scouts, is that they begin to decide when and where they'll hit the various schools they're scheduled to scout that fall. I was under the impression this was all mapped out by the Director of College Scouting, but this does not seem to be the case.

As for GMs, it's an entirely different proposition. At the executive level, there's a lot more work getting done. One source's list included:

- Set up early boards for the next fall college evaluations.

- Seniors and juniors to watch for.

- Watch previous season's tape on the aforementioned.

- Tag players who scouts had as draftable or priority free agents (PFAs) who didn't get to sign or make it through OTAs (excluding injuries).

- Evaluate the players that have finished two seasons (to grade scouts).

- Reach out to college tree on who they like in their conference as *real* guys - not their own teams.

- Early prep on upcoming unrestricted free agents. Make sure who is in the last year, along with potential cap cuts, contract voidable, etc.

- Potential trades and looking at excess on other teams' rosters.

- Thin spots by team.

- Media comments on camp/OTA performances.

I guess the bottom line is that schedules vary, but even workaholics need a little time to reset so their brains don't turn to mush.

An old scout discusses the job

My friend Danton Barto was an area scout for the St. Louis Rams from 2013-17. Barto is unique in that he's an old-school football guy. A college linebacker, he retains that mentality. His lack of polish really cuts through the bull and makes him fun to talk to.

The best part about Danton is he's all killer and no filler. For a time, Danton wrote scouting reports on draft prospects for agents through my service, Inside the League. Danton's reports were always very brief and to the point. At times, that made them a little tough to sell to contract advisers who were used to receiving more buzzwords and excessive details. Danton's reports were basic: '"this guy is good and this is why," or "this guy won't make it, and this is why." A few concise paragraphs covered it. What's more, he was rarely wrong.

This is why I invited him to speak to our staff at the 2018 College Gridiron Showcase in the Dallas area. He had so many gems that I've presented his talk almost in its entirety here. Enjoy.

"That's the hard part about scouting, guys. It's a business. You're going to get to know some of these kids through the process, and you like them. Like (2016 Bills second-round LB) Reggie Ragland and I are still great friends. I love Reg. I see Reggie at the Alabama games, and he'll come visit me and talk to my son. I love Reggie. I'm a fan of Reggie Ragland. I just like the dude. You hit it off with certain guys. You become close to them. You like them. You like the way they do things. There's guys like that.

"You know what I do in character? It's gotten, when I was with (Rams GM Les Snead) and them, (head coach Jeff) Fisher and them knew I did my work. So, they'd ask, 'Barto, what about this kid?' (gives the thumbs-up). That's it. I'd say, 'what do you want to know?' Because if he's a turd, I'm going to tell you. If I do this (gives thumbs down), they'd go, 'oh, geez, coach, hold on.' He's dumb, he can't learn, he smokes weed every day. Guys, let me tell you something: they all smoke weed. For us older guys, that's our beer of their generation. These kids all smoke weed, and they all fail the tests, and they all fail tests at the highest levels. And first-rounders, don't kid yourself. Guys, you wouldn't believe the failed tests."

Barto was asked why Ole Miss OT Laremy Tunsil slid after the infamous video of him smoking marijuana was released on draft day.

"There was more than that, and I don't want to go into it, but Tunsil's got a *lot* of stuff going on, a lot of wildness going on around him, and you hope that he picks it up and fixes it," Barto said. "He's been clean (since he's been in the league). He hasn't been popped. The guy's in his prime. It's the same as (then-Rams cornerback) Janoris Jenkins. 'Jackrabbit.' He's one of my favorite dudes in the world. I love Rabbit. Jesus Christ, Rabbit failed out of (the University of) Florida, kicked out, went to North Alabama. Rabbit's never failed a drug test ever (with the Rams). Now, you telling me Rabbit doesn't smoke weed? I'm betting he probably does it all the time. But he's learned to keep himself clean. He loves football. The first thing you notice about Rabbit, when I came to the Rams, is that he loves football.

"You better know, who you're scouting, you better figure that out immediately -- does this dude love football? And here's another thing just to tell you, because I've explained this to guys in our team that never played professionally to help them understand. There's three guys in every locker room. There's the guy that plays football for money. That's all he cares about, and I've seen them be super-successful. There's the guy who plays football because of everything that goes with football: the girls, the glamor, the glitz, hanging out, 'I'm a football player.' I've seen that guy be successful. Then the last guy is the guy that loves football, right? Better hope you have enough of those guys, but I've seen every one of those guys be successful. But that's what sits in your locker.

"You have to remember something guys. On the pro side, those are millionaires, and sometimes it's mind-boggling because you get used to being around them. The colleges now are kissing these kids' asses. It's ridiculous. It's unbelievable at times, and I'm like, 'good God, how do you do college coaching now?' You've got to kiss this kid's butt, and you've got kids announcing that he got signed, and God blessed me, and the Lord praise me, I got a thing in Alabama. That's the time that we live in now. We've got to start understanding they are young kids, right? They make mistakes, man. Kids make mistakes. When you were 18, 19, most of us were pretty damn (dumb), right? We probably all did something stupid that we didn't get caught for, thank God. So, I tried to give guys the benefit of the doubt.

"When you're interviewing, and things of that nature, you have the answers (to the questions you're going to ask) most of the time. There's two ways to attack that, and I've seen it attacked both ways. I've seen (scouts) attack guys, be kind of buttholes about it. Like, they know he failed (a drug) test. I tell them, look, before they answer these questions . . . I'm going to tell them, you've got to be honest. We already have the answers. I'm not the cops. I'm not condemning you if you smoke weed. Whoop-tee-do! Are you still smoking weed? Do you have a problem with it? And if you do, how much do you smoke? When are you smoking? I mean, we can sit there and judge them, but guys do bad things at times. The GM is making a judgment call on the character of players, because at a certain round, everybody's buying them, and don't think they're not. Because if a guy lasts in the seventh round, and he's a third-round talent, somebody's ass is drafting him, and going, '(hey) I'll take the risk.'

"That's what you've got to learn in your scouting department is, you're a team, and you've got to learn to be a team and protect each other's ass. We want to get the guy right, but I don't want to one-up you. So, let's work together. If I hear something, I'm going to be like, 'Steve, hey, you need to check this story out on this kid. You've been into investigating this kid?' 'Yeah, I went there, I didn't hear it.' 'Call somebody else because I'm hearing this, OK?' And that's what good teams do."

All-star games: A prospect's safety net

Scouting and evaluation is a crapshoot. It's very inexact, no matter what teams and draft gurus tell you. Obviously, I'm a believer in the work scouts do, and I believe they hit far more often than they miss. At the same time, all-star games provide a key platform for those players scouts miss on, and no matter how hard scouts work, they miss sometimes. Especially at running back, a position that's been pretty devalued over the years.

One back who went undrafted but had some success in the league was Khiry Robinson, who, though never a star, still spent four years in the league. Justin VanFulpen is an agent today, but in 2013, he was assembling the rosters for the Texas vs. The Nation college all-star game. Justin invited Robinson to the game in Allen, Texas, just outside Dallas.

"I remember seeing highlights of him and liked his running style, but all the scouts I talked to get a buy-in called him a JAG (just a guy). He was the last running back to be added, and one reason I even added him was because I needed another Texas running back. I only had one small-time agent calling me about him. Can't even remember the guy's name. He had good stats and looked the part, and he was very humble when I invited him, and he accepted right away. He thought it was too good to be true, and he thanked me a ton for the opportunity.

"He was able to go in that week of practice and outshine D.J. Harper from Boise State, Matthew Tucker from TCU and Ronnie Wingo from Arkansas, and be the best running back on the Texas side. Only (Saints RB) Latavius Murray from UCF has had a better career so far in the NFL. Scouts liked the fact that he ran hard, but still didn't sign him as a (priority free agent). He had to go to the Saints as a tryout guy, then ended up getting a chance to sign. I was surprised he didn't sign as a priority free agent, so I checked in with him a day after the draft and he told me he got a tryout."

Even though Robinson once shared a backfield with Cam Newton (while at Blinn College in Bryan, Texas), he barely registered with NFL teams while bouncing from Mesabi Range Community College to Blinn to West Texas A&M. But his play at the TVN game sparked something, and years later, he became part of an NFL backfield. However, it's doubtful he even gets a tryout if he didn't go to Allen at Justin's request.

Finding sleepers

If there's one question I always get, not only from my newer agent clients but also from my more seasoned ones, it's "how do you find a sleeper?" Where are the seniors who come out of nowhere, climb the charts over the last weeks of the season, test well and wind up on NFL rosters?

I can't say I have the answer to that. In fact, one year at the combine, I had lunch with one of the more seasoned scouts in the game, a great guy and a great friend. I asked him this question, and he didn't really have an answer, either. In discussing it with him, my takeaway was that most teams spend about two-thirds of their time on the guys who'll be taken in the top third of the draft roughly, i.e., rounds 1-3. Most teams see these guys as the real difference-makers, the players that will make or break their rosters, so they want to spend an inordinate amount of time on these particular players. The ones who go in rounds 4-7 -- most typically the players we'd characterize as sleepers -- aren't seen as players who will help you win titles. They may be solid starters in time, and might even develop into stars, but the risk isn't worth the reward, generally. Teams get busy, they can't apply the resources to evaluating everybody, and players fall through the cracks.

So, what's the best way to find guys that are "under the radar" or "off the grid?" Here's my take on it.

- One way is to find players who were at junior colleges who don't have a lengthy body of work at the four-year college level and bloom late. I know there is very little evaluation done at the JC level, mostly because players don't go from a juco to the draft very often.

- A second way is to find a college basketball player who just switched to football (i.e., Jimmy Graham, who played in New Orleans, Seattle, Green Bay and Chicago, or San Diego's Antonio Gates).

- Another way is to find players who didn't play football until college, or very little high school ball, especially if they came from other countries (a la former Detroit first-rounder Zeke Ansah or Indy first-rounder Bjoern Woerner, or even Oakland second-rounder Menelik Watson, all from the '13 draft class).

- A fourth way is to find guys who switched to impact positions late (usually before their senior seasons, but maybe even mid-season). These are typically tight ends who move to tackle, or maybe defensive tackles who move to guard, or whatever. Less frequently, you find running backs or wide receivers who move to cornerback, or even QBs who move to wide receiver. But all of these qualify.

- The fifth way is to find a good player at an un-sexy position – he's good, but not high-impact – who plays either in the far Northeast (Maine/New Hampshire/Rhode Island, etc.) or the Southwest/Mountain West (West Texas, Utah, Nevada, New Mexico, Idaho, Montana and the Dakotas).

- A sixth way is to find pure track stars who will "test out of the gym," but who aren't really refined football players yet. Former LSU kick returner Trindon Holliday, who went in the sixth round of the 2010 draft, is an example of this. He never developed much beyond being a kick returner and gimmick player despite going to the U.S. Olympic Trials in 2008.

- Small-school teams that don't have a winning tradition are always overlooked, both by scouts and agents. Sometimes you can find a diamond in the rough, though convincing teams that you've got a guy won't be easy.

There may be other ways. I know no one has the 'patent' on this, but these seem to be the patterns for most players who come out of nowhere, figuratively speaking, and enjoy NFL success.

No experience required

It's been my theory that scouting has changed in the last 10 years, with more of a focus on what happens off the field and less on pure production. In other words, despite what scouts and executives love to say, the NFL Combine and pro days are more important than ever, and 40 times, media buzz and "it factor" are a bigger part of Draft Day than ever.

This really came home to me when I was having lunch with a scouting friend of mine. When I started discounting many of this year's top picks as one-year wonders, he countered that the players I suggested as alternates were *also* one-year wonders. That got me thinking: do teams really value the kind of production and staying power they used to value? It's something I wanted to take a look at, but how do you measure such a thing?

I wanted to try, so I gave my intern a project: take the top 50 picks from 2017 and put them alongside the top 50 from 10 years ago (2008), and give me a line about the season *before* their last season in college (for the '17 draft, 2015; for the '08 draft, 2006). In other words, I wanted to see what kind of resume they'd accumulated before catching fire, becoming a 'star' in the eyes of the media, and possibly riding the hype train to first-round status. My goal -- determine how many "one-year wonders" made it to the first round in 2017 and compare it to the totals from 10 years ago.

My conclusion: to get drafted in the first round 10 years ago, it was pretty simple. You had played *at least* two straight seasons in good health, at the same position where you were drafted. You had started every game for two years, no questions asked. Also, you might have come from a small conference or a lesser school, but you were highly decorated there. Finally, in most cases, you had four seasons of college football under your belt.

These days, all bets are off. Here are a few thoughts based on what we found:

- More and more top picks might have arrived at school with a nice pedigree, but they just don't have a lot of experience (and certainly far fewer games started) before having a big season that vaults them into the draft discussion (and often, into the draft).

- Program means way more, too; Ohio State players just seem to be tinged with gold as teams seem to value the teams Urban Meyer and Ryan Day have assembled over the years. The same could be said for Michigan and Jim Harbaugh.

- Of course, there are more juniors to choose from, which tilts selection in the direction of less experience and fewer honors (and more projection on the part of scouts). In 2008, 29 seniors went in the first 50 picks versus only 18 last year.

- The biggest revelation, however, is the number of players who started fewer than 10 games in the year before their last college season.

Based on these criteria, I would argue that, due to health or inexperience, 14 players who went Top-50 in 2017 would never have been picked so highly 10 years before. Here are their names, followed by their round and overall selections: Bears QB Mitch Trubisky (1/2); Bengals WR John Ross (1/9); Saints CB Marshon Lattimore (1/11); Indianapolis SS Malik Hooker (1/15); Broncos OT Garrett Bolles (1/20); Falcons DE Takkarist McKinley (1/26); Cowboys DE Taco Charlton (1/28); Browns TE David Njoku (1/29); Steelers OLB T.J. Watt (1/30); Saints OT Ryan Ramczyk (1/32); Panthers WR Curtis Samuel (1/40); Colts CB Quincy Wilson (1/46); Ravens OLB Tyus Bowser (1/47); and Bucs SS Justin Evans (1/50). Of that group, I'd call Lattimore, Watt, Ramczyk and Samuel the only stars in the group.

Granted, the nature of football has changed, and colleges have followed the NFL in using a much more aggressive rotation system (especially at running back and on the defensive line), and that affects things. What's more, the players who would have stuck around four years in the past leave early these days. Still, the change of philosophy in favor of risk has been, to me, unmistakable.

How a small-school DB got to the NFL

Bill Schwenk (who's no longer an agent) had only been in player representation a month when, during the 2011 season, he noticed a cornerback at Nicholls State in Thibodaux, La., named Bobby

Felder. Felder had played alongside Nicholls State CB Lardarius Webb, who went 3/88 to the Ravens in 2009. Webb and Schwenk had a mutual friend, and this friend insisted to Schwenk that Felder was a player.

Felder had compiled big-time stats during his college career, but received no interest from agents and only minimal attention from scouts. Though Felder had logged 190 tackles in three years, along with five picks, eight passes broken up, 12 passes defensed, 49 tackles, two forced fumbles, two fumble recoveries and three blocked kicks during his senior season, he was missed.

How come? Maybe because Thibodaux is in swamp country in south Louisiana; Nicholls' main claim to fame is that every summer it is home to Manning Passing Academy. However, it was by no means a football factory, having gone 1-10 in 2011 and 4-7 in 2010. The fact that the team won only one game his senior season didn't do anything to help Felder create buzz. In addition, Felder wasn't written up by either of the scouting combines, National and BLESTO, going into the season. That was likely because the school didn't bother to have a junior day, the time when the combines come in to time, weigh and measure possible prospects. If a team were to have found him, it would have had to actually go to campus and check him out, or at least see him in a road game. It's easy for a player to develop a rap as non-athletic when no one has a 40 time on him, and lack of speed at cornerback is the kiss of death.

It turns out that only three teams made it to Nicholls that season: Seattle, Oakland and Atlanta. Seemingly, none were all that impressed (though the Falcons met with Schwenk at the Senior Bowl to discuss Felder). Later, Schwenk asked a friendly scout why only three teams had made it to Thibodaux. "Honestly, they're lazy!" was the response. The scout told Bill that because Felder played at lowly and remote Nicholls State, scouts knew few GMs would ask about the school or its players. That meant they could cut the school out of their route, and most did.

At any rate, Schwenk was a believer, and he continued to recruit Felder. He only got competition from one other agent, a veteran who heard of Felder very late and tried to get through to him through the cornerback's brother-in-law. Schwenk staved off the older agent and signed Felder, but making believers of NFL teams wasn't easy. That's why he made a game film and started to send it out to teams.

One of the scouts who saw his film was then-Green Bay scout Alonzo Highsmith, who's known in the business for his keen eye and excellent insights (he's now with Seattle). Highsmith went directly to GM Ted Thompson and told him he had found a sleeper.

From there, word started to get out, and by the end of February, there was buzz around Felder. It reached such a fever pitch that when the school scheduled its pro day, many NFL scouts called to request that it be rescheduled to be held the day before LSU's pro day so they could make both workouts. Alas, at his big day, he ran in the 4.6 range, turning most evaluators off. Only one team retained interest: Minnesota. The next day, Schwenk drove Felder to Baton Rouge to meet the Vikings' scout and defensive backs coach after LSU's pro day.

Felders' chances were almost extinguished; when he was passed over on draft day, the Vikings were the only team that called. Schwenk quickly signed Felder to a contract as an undrafted free agent, and the Colonel beat overwhelming odds and made the roster. He wound up spending parts of three seasons with the Vikings, Bucs and Bills.

Anyway, the point is not that the NFL almost overlooked a poor man's Deion Sanders. It's just that it's one more illustration that there are still sleepers, and there are scouts (and agents) who are willing to trust their instincts and look for players in out-of-the-way places.

More thoughts and insights on scouting

"Measurements are part of (a player's) ability. I don't think you can separate the two. Everything else being equal, skills and production, your bigger, faster, stronger, quicker player is always better. Part of (a player's) ability is his height, weight, speed and athleticism. You can't really separate those two. Are there small players that have made it in the league? Yes, but they're the exception, not the rule. The usual rule in the NFL when you draft a small player is, it turns out to be regretful. There's a lyric to a folk song -- I like folk singers -- that there's no profit in regret. So, if somebody drafts a small player, and it's regretful, they're not going to draft another small player. They're not going to make it habit. You know, I have drafted small players, and usually it's regrettable. Especially shorter offensive linemen, unless they have exceptionally long arms, they can't win that battle. They get covered up. They can win occasionally, but they can't win it enough to get to that second contract."

"I would say the most critical time for your players in interviews is in the all-star games and on campus. Those are the ones you want to prepare them for. Every club treats the combine differently. Believe me, I've invested a lot of time in my life tracking the combine interviews. When I was Director of College Scouting, I always liked those interviews, and I got so into the moment that all I remember is questions. I don't remember any responses, OK? It was my job to ask the questions, and it was somebody else's job to write down the answer. It was just so trying to set the athlete up so hard that you'd miss the responses that we needed to know. I never got a feel for the athlete. Somebody had to tell me what their feeling was. So, what I've learned over the years is that, at the combine, all you're trying to do is get a feel for them. it's 12 minutes, OK? It's 12 minutes. All you're trying to do is, you're just trying to get to know them. Now, some clubs would put the pressure on them and call them out, OK? I've been there. I've done that, and what it usually does is, it kills the player for the coaches to take responses that way. It's a lot sounder to wait on those players that have issues different coaches would be concerned about and to bring them in for the top 30 visits where they can actually get to know the athlete, and they're not trying to jam them up to see if they'll break, OK? So, for a lot of clubs it's just about, 'hey, tell me about who you are, let's talk.' That's what it got to be for us at the combine. I just wanted our coaches to be introduced to the players. It was their first exposure.

"I would say one thing that is a big pet peeve of mine: once the process starts for interviews and (every team's 30 in-person visits), keep your athlete out of the media. Don't have them tell people who you visit. Don't tell a local reporter that your client visited the Chicago Bears or Denver Broncos because you have violated trust. We were very explicit in our letters to agents, and verbally on the phone with numerous reminders, that we do not want your visit publicized. We may have done visits that got out before we got there, but there's only one way it got out: it either came from the athlete or it came from the agent. It's the most competitive sport in the world, OK? You don't want to flash everybody what your intentions are about your top 30 visits. We usually drafted people off their top 30 visits, so we weren't real happy when they got out. So, you're helping, in terms of developing a trust relationship with an organization and a team, you not giving it out, you get high marks. That means a lot to us. That's a trust thing. We can work together to be messengers in everything, because it's very important to keep that part from the media. It's funny. Sometimes, we have tracked it down, and it's the athlete sitting in a locker room back at his college in Wisconsin talking to his buddies. And he's like, 'yeah I just went to the Bears,' and it's that athlete's buddy who tells his agent, and that agent feeds it to the press. We know it's not always the fault of the player's agent, or the player, but you just have to learn to play fair with everybody. It helps everyone in the process.

"What's more important, college production, or NFL upside? I really don't know how to answer that one. College production depends on the level of play and competition. You know, it could be one year if this guy's a senior, had 15 sacks, and was part of a very competitive conference. Sometimes, you look at all those athletes and read who (they're playing against), and you say, well, those aren't NFL players. It doesn't mean anything. So, for that player, his NFL upside in terms of the skillset that he represents that is intangible, will be more important.

"NFL upside, skills, height, weight, speed and athletic skills and positional skills are more important than college production. Being able to project that athlete to do the things that he can do at the next level is very important. We had a perfect example in Chicago about two years ago. We drafted Cornelius Washington from Georgia. He was an unbelievable physical specimen with very little college production. He hadn't done a whole lot of growth, but we knew we were going to be patient with him. Then he started coming on and having a little production. When he did it right, he could do it at a high level. He had NFL upside at 6-6, 280, 4.54 forty, long arms, strong, powerful, yet very little college production. So, somebody like that in the sixth round over somebody that played at Michigan and had 150 tackles, but he had limited athleticism, you probably won't take him on his production alone." -- **Falcons national scout Phil Emery, who has also scouted for the Bears and Chiefs and served as Chicago's GM from 2012-14**

"Texans GM Charley Casserly had this great system, and we had great college scouts. I was on the pro side of it at the time, and we had good pro scouts. We had a really good staff, but we were what you'd call a scout-driven organization. The scouts made the decision on the picks. Denver, on the other hand, and this was kind of a difference of philosophies, they were more of a coach-driven organization. That is, they would have scouts, and they'd come in, and they'd give them information from what they found out from the film work and the visitations at the schools and such. But the coaches would then take the film and do the evaluations, and so the coaches kind of made the picks in the draft." – **Miller McCalmon, former Bills and Oilers assistant coach and former Redskins, Lions and Texans scout**

"I know if you are a good scout, then all other outside influences (i.e., media) will not impact one's opinion. Scouts are paid well and paid for 'their opinion.' Stick to it, right or wrong. You are trying to make your team the best it can be, and most GMs or head coaches do not want 'yes' people. (However,) I have been around a few that would (pay attention to internet scouts and media) and who have been influenced tremendously by what mock drafts say, and have gotten themselves and the organization in trouble. Those individuals in the media, etc., get their information from somewhere. Most of the time it comes from someone in an organization. Those individuals don't know what your team needs are and what your emphasis is on a position. They could be wrong, not know the rest of the country and how a player stacks up against others, medical history or mental issues. So why would you listen to it or let it sway your opinion? Trust in your scouts; and scouts, trust in your ability to evaluate players. The other is best left for the armchair QB." – **Mike Murphy, former area scout, Seahawks, Chiefs, Dolphins and Giants**

"(Sharing info with other teams' scouts) was a fine line. That was a very, very fine line of how to do things. You're told, certainly, you can't let a lot of information out from your team, but at the same time, maybe it was a guy that could get information from a coach at the school that he knew that was in our area. We could kinda use that and work with that, without giving up any team secrets. It's a very fine line, and it's really kinda hard to explain, I guess, but we'd talk. I think there's a line somewhere and you have to know where it is. Every team had one. Do I think that it made the some of the management guys a little nervous sometimes? Probably so, but they do the same thing. That's just the nature of the business without giving up a lot of team secrets like who you're drafting, or who you're looking at. But all you have to do is pay attention. It's kinda hard to hide anything these days." – **James Jefferson, former Seahawks safety and Saints area scout**

"Every player, coach, parent and agent needs to know that the bigger the stage, the bigger the impact in regards to how a player is viewed during the evaluation process. Ninety percent of all NFL personnel (and I, as well) consider three factors to be extra-special during evaluation. These are: level of competition; how recent the contest was; and the importance of the game. This is true whether you're evaluating high school players for college or college players for the NFL. When a scout makes his school visit and is making his film decisions, usually he wants to watch the most recent competition against the best-available competition. Many will go back to the previous season if there is a bowl game or a big rivalry match-up (Alabama-Auburn, Ohio State-Michigan) to scrutinize how well an athlete performs under the most intense circumstances. It matters a lot how well players perform 'under the big lights.' The other huge factor is how well a player performs versus the best competition. Let's say a defensive end has a ton of sacks and tackles for loss throughout the season, but doesn't show up in a matchup with a highly regarded offensive tackle who's an NFL prospect himself. That could really affect his grade. Like him or not, former Texas A&M QB Johnny Manziel came up big most of the time versus the top competition. For example, he generated a record 516 total yards versus Oklahoma in the 2013 Cotton Bowl. People like to pick apart the couple of games when he was banged up or playing in poor weather and didn't put up numbers, but he did more than enough versus Alabama and other great teams to warrant a high draft choice. (His failure in the NFL wasn't) because of a lack of talent or moxie. Obviously, a player's entire body of work is considered during the evaluation process. Still, when the 'brass' (head coach, coordinator, GM, Director of College Scouting and, in some cases, the owner) wants to take a look at a prospect, games under the brightest lights possible are usually in highest demand." – **Ken Moll, former Browns and Jaguars area scout**

"One thing (fans) don't understand is – (though) height, weight, and speed are important, I'm not going to lie – you have to have athletic ability and you better have instinctive characteristics as a player. Fans may not understand that nothing beats what the film shows. I say that prefacing a very important point. How many times have you seen a guy who didn't fit any characteristics you were looking for, but he was a football player? And how many times did those people make it? They're littered throughout the league. I would say that's the biggest thing that you have to look at. Finally, the hardest thing to do is look at the guy's mentality toward the game, his temperament. Everybody thinks they can judge it. Everybody can see he has all the will, but that's not measurable. Your best scouts understand what that guy brings without even saying a word to him, based upon what they've seen in the past." – **Matt Boockmeier, Edmonton Eskimos area scout and former Packers and Saints area scout**

"A lot of fans think we pick it up at the combine, but we've actually been watching guys for two years sometimes. It's a process. We've been gathering information on these guys for 18 months, but it's not just what the guys did at the combine. The risers and fallers thing is kind of a farce in a sense. It's a piece of the puzzle, but it's not the whole picture. A lot of times, the background that comes out a week before or a day before has been known for months. Size, speed and production are all keys, but also character, being able to fit in the scheme and intelligence. It's way more complicated than the actual fan realizes. There's a lot of hours that go into these decisions. It's very rarely a gut feeling. It's more programmed and thought out. A lot of guys think we picked this guy just because Mel Kiper liked him. And just because Mel Kiper likes a guy and a team doesn't like the guy, it doesn't make the team wrong. I have all of the respect in the world for Mel Kiper, but they are not talking to position coaches, they aren't talking to parents, they are not talking to high school coaches. I've talked to their high school teachers before. It's very in-depth, especially when it's a guy who could be drafted in the top two or three rounds. You reach out to tons of people to try and get a good picture on who the kid is. You can evaluate the player off of the tape, but at the same time, if you are drafting a guy in the first round, he will be attached to your franchise forever, so there's a lot of pressure on those picks. There's so much that goes into it. It's more than he threw for 4,000 yards and ran a 4.4 at the combine. I don't think people really appreciate how much work goes into the evaluation process." – **Marcus Hendrickson, Director of Player Personnel at Minnesota and former Dolphins and Browns area scout**

"The biggest misconception is (that creating a scouting profile for a prospect is not) a two-to-three-year process, instead of just the hot name. The time that is invested . . . no one really has a concept of (and) how much digging we have to do on that. Fans are usually like, 'how did you not know that?' It's about building relationships at the schools and getting to know the players without doing illegal activity. It's underlooked." – **Scott Aligo, Director of Player Personnel at Michigan State and former Browns area scout**

"There's a lot more that goes into it other than, 'is he a good player?' What might be a great player for the Miami Dolphins might not be the best player for the Pittsburgh Steelers. It's about understanding the fit. It's not just about how good a player is, it's how does he fit in the culture? Does he fit in our scheme? Questions like that, you have to answer." – **Redskins (and former Browns) area scout Harrison Ritcher**

"An area scout is going to go into a school three times. There's going to be another guy who goes in there twice, and there's probably going to be another person who goes to a game. There are hundreds of hours dedicated to a single player taken in the draft regardless if it's first round, fifth round or undrafted. They are putting in the work, not only to figure out who the player is on the field, but also off the field. I think fans see a 6-foot-5 player who is 250 pounds and had 10 sacks and automatically think he should be a first-round pick. Well, maybe he shouldn't be. Maybe he doesn't have the instincts, or the strength, or the explosion that we look for. Maybe he's bad off of the field. I don't think your average NFL fan has a full scope of understanding what all goes in to projecting a player in the NFL." – **Matt Lindsey, General Manager at Ole Miss and former Philadelphia Eagles college scouting coordinator**

"We really want to know who (prospects) are. The tape is one thing because it's so accessible, and you can watch it from anywhere on the planet as long as you have Wi-Fi on your iPad. That's going to be there, and there is plenty of time to watch the tape. But going into the school, talking to them, finding out contacts, going to the guy's high school and talking to people who grew up with them and talking to his family down the stretch . . . people don't realize how much goes into that to really figure out who is this guy -- not only who we will invest money in, but someone who we will let join our organization. A lot of resources are put into that. Psychologically. Background information. Who is this guy? Does he love football? I don't think (fans) understand the magnitude of what goes into it." – **Morocco Brown, Colts Director of College Scouting; he has also served on the scouting staffs of the Bears, Redskins and Browns**

"A big thing for me while learning to scout with the Falcons and (head coach) Dan Reeves was character, work ethic and production. Kids that have lots of production in college usually can do the same on the next level, if given a chance. Brent Grimes . . . a free agent from (Division II) Shippensburg University, signed with the Falcons after the '06 draft. I saw this kid on my last school visit of the year in 2005 (after they finished 4-7), and I was awestruck by his talent from a small school, and I promised to do whatever to get him in front of the Falcons. I traveled to his pro day on a cold day in February of '06, and he ran a 4.5 (40) on a basketball court and had a vertical of 41 (inches) using the wall. (His) backpedal was smooth and (his) breaks were sudden, and (his) ball skills were incredible, along with his hand-eye coordination. He was also a punt returner on his level, with the ability to make defenders miss. Just very athletic, with bend, balance and body control for a small-school football player. His only flaw, to me, was his height, but he made it up with his vertical. He was not really into school, but he knew football, and that set him apart. The Falcons coaches questioned his speed, but they marveled at his playmaking ability. First day at rookie camp, he steps on the field and made an incredible play, and the rest is history. My favorite all-time player that I scouted." – **Bruce Plummer, former Falcons area scout**

CHAPTER 6
On Character

E very year at the combine, we hold a big seminar and invite all our clients. I try to bring in a speaker from the football world who is informative and entertaining. In 2016, that person was former Browns GM Ray Farmer, who's a draft consultant for the Rams now.

I had breakfast with him the day of the seminar. In the course of our conversation, we got to talking about how teams gauge character during the evaluation process, and he said some things that I thought were very interesting. Farmer said that if you're dealing with a player who's a major character risk, there are two things you must do. No. 1, you must have someone who can be his confidante/manager. You have to find someone, either on the team or from his family or from his hometown, who takes responsibility for him getting to meetings on time, keeping him out of the headlines or otherwise keeping his nose clean. The model for this is Randy Moss and his brother, Eric, whom the Vikings kept on the roster during Moss' early days just to make sure he stayed on course.

No. 2, if you're going to take a character risk, you have to be able to pair that player with others at his position who are good influences. In other words, if he's a cornerback, you only take him if your other DBs are good citizens. If he's a QB, you make sure your other passers are strait-laced. If he's a rookie, make sure he's the only rookie in that situation. If he's from Ohio State, make sure your other Buckeyes are good guys. Don't take a chance on making waves that could rock the team.

Farmer closed with this thought. NFL teams have dozens of players who are questionable, character-wise. Every single team is standing on the ledge, blindfolded, hoping there's no false step. One false move, and the team could be headed into the abyss. It's just the reality of the game. No team is completely safe.

What you don't know may hurt you

At the 2018 College Gridiron Showcase, former Rams scout Barto was one of the presenters, and he was asked about the situation with former LSU OT La'el Collins, whose pregnant girlfriend was murdered shortly before the 2015 draft. Collins went from a potential first-rounder to an undrafted free agent who wound up signing with the Cowboys.

Barto's answer made it clear that teams had questions that couldn't be found in media reports.

"It was a double murder," Barto said. "The media, you've got to understand, the media is crazy for all this information. We get all this great information now, but you've got to understand something. I tell people all the time -- the media's got a job to do, to create stories, right? Half the stuff that's been put out there is (expletive). Why do you think the NFL always says . . . we're doing our own investigation, right? Because you don't know if it's true or not. Now sometimes we do know, and they're like. 'oh (expletive), this is bad.' There's two things you don't want to do, is embarrass your team, or embarrass 'the shield.'"

Barto said even he is surprised by what his own team's security staff dug up on prospects.

"We (had) a guy on our staff at the Rams, OK? He's been a cop, he's been an FBI guy and all he does is travel the country," Barto said. "When I'm traveling, he's traveling the country going and visiting your home town. He's visiting your coach, your police if you know them, he's going to find everything there is to know about you. Sometimes it shocks me what he finds. It's information I could have never gotten, that nobody knew. And most of the time, he'll be, like, do you know about this?"

Here's another take on how to resolve character questions on draft day.

"As far as character goes, all I'm going to say is, talent rules the day," said Falcons national scout Phil Emery. "There's a lot of talk in the media about teams making decisions based on character. Did we skip players over character? Absolutely, but there is a difference between convictions and charges, OK? That's practical. There is a difference between making mistakes, and having matured, and not making repetitive mistakes, and people that never change. Part of that decision process for people in personnel and coaching is to make those decisions.

"But at the end of the day, if that player is on your board . . . you're going to take him. Talent rules the day. I always say, when we get into those arguments is, do you want to play with him or against him? Because if he doesn't play for the Bears, he's probably going to be playing for the Vikings, you know? He's going to probably be playing for Green Bay, or he might go to New York, and he might be on our schedule, so with him or without him? You have to have enough information to have convictions in that decision."

At the same time, take too many gambles and you could be out of a job, Emery added.

"You're going to have to take a risk, OK?" Emery said. "Now, if you take too many risks, you end up digging a hole there is no way to dig out of. It happens. It's just part of the process. But in terms of taking players. . . I would say, if a prospect has had more than one conviction, and it's a serious offense, you're going to have a hard time. If it's domestic abuse . . . and if it's happened repetitively, you're really going to be hurting. The league has stepped in in a way that I've never seen before in terms of the follow-up. I don't know if anybody remembers when (former Miami free safety) Brandon Meriweather was a prospect in the league. The league had stepped in and told everybody that they weren't going to tolerate (domestic abuse), and wanted us to take less risks, basically not taking upon us as much risk on guys that had documented mischief. But Brandon was drafted in the first round because when you look at a draft board, when you go through all those players, there are far more players that have issues or concerns that you have to talk through than ones that don't. Why? Because they're people, OK? We all carry baggage."

The fact that character is a relative thing is echoed by former Falcons area scout Bruce Plummer.

"(Character) depends on the team and what they can deal with," he said. "Remember, you are bringing this player to a new city with lots of temptations. Every team has a different set of rules. Some GMs and owners allow certain things, and others don't. Once the decision is made, it's too late to say, damn!"

Bad apples and the supplemental draft

Finding supplemental draft success stories isn't easy. It's been quite a while since the "supp draft" was turning out players like Miami's Bernie Kosar and Steve Walsh, Ohio State's Cris Carter, Alabama's Bobby Humphrey and Syracuse's Rob Moore in the late 1980s. Since then, there have been solid players here and there but no consistency. In fact, the only one that really stands out in the past decade is Baylor's Josh Gordon, who, ahem, turned out to have off-field issues.

It made me wonder if all – or a high percentage at least – of the players who wind up on the post-draft scrap heap have obvious off-field warts, since so few ever get drafted and fewer still make a real impact. I reached out to six active scouts with just that question. Their answers mostly confirmed my thesis, though some were mixed.

- One scout said that in the "75-90 percent range" of rejection cases, it's either character or an NCAA-related issue, such as a player who was waiting on an eligibility ruling that came in late.

- Another scout said most supplemental draft prospects are "not necessarily bad people," though he allowed that sometimes such players *are* bad apples.

- One strongly disagreed, calling my thesis way too broad. "I've never seen a study, but personally I don't believe that would be a very factual statement," he said. This scout indicated that he feels most players in the supplemental draft are victims of circumstances beyond their control.

- Another agreed with me, confirming that it's "usually the case" that the player in question has off-field problems that are significant.

- The final one I corresponded with said he wouldn't say 90 percent had character issues, but said probably half did. "Lots of warts with supplemental drafting," he admitted.

I guess the reason most teams pass on supplemental draft prospects is more because they don't make the grade on the field, rather than off the field. As always, however, character goes into each evaluation, and might tip the balance. How much is hard to determine.

More insights on how to weigh character

"Determining who's draftable varies. With the Chiefs, our system was really derived from the Patriots system, so character really mattered. There are players that fit you playing-wise but they're not character fits. That's important, because guys get taken off the board all the time. If you value character, or if you value (more) playing-wise, each team has to decide that. Each team could look at the same player and see them 32 different ways. Character is no different. We pulled several players out due to character every year. There were first-round guys who wouldn't necessarily be a character fit for us, and their card was thrown out. Teams most serious about (character) are the Patriots, the Falcons and everyone that came from the New England system. Those teams are usually sticklers for character -- they just know there are different levels of character issues. If a guy had any issues with females or hit a girl, he would never be in our building, but if guys had failed a few (drug) tests . . .

the truth is, everyone in the league smokes (marijuana), so it comes down to how your GM values character as opposed to ability. I can assure you that we took several guys off the board strictly for character. It really comes down to, in my opinion, the type of relationship the GM has with his subordinates. If there are guys he trusts, he may have a different level of trust as opposed to a guy who just came in the last year. I think ultimately it comes down to the nature of the relationship between the head coach, GM, Director of Player Personnel and the Director of College Scouting." – **Aundrae Harris, former Chiefs area scout**

"After doing my research, I knew this kid (Syracuse SS Tanard Jackson, drafted 4/106 by Tampa Bay in '07) had some issues with marijuana and had some failed drug tests in college. While interviewing him, I was straightforward, and he denied he had a problem. Well, to make a long story short, he was drafted. And (he became a starter) until his troubles with substance abuse started. In 2010, he was suspended indefinitely by the NFL for a second positive test. While trying out for another team, he was again suspended for substance issues. One of my big things was to always have good sources at the schools on my call list, because they know the history, both on and off the field, of these kids. I told the Falcons, 'Don't touch this kid with a 10-foot pole.' Another player, through our research, we knew of pictures of this player flashing money with guns and posing with champagne bottles at a party and many other (times). I knew about the photos, but the player denied they existed. He was even asked by the coaching staff, and he again denied it and said there are no pictures. He was not touched by the Falcons. He was drafted, but did not play long because of his troubles." – **Bruce Plummer, former Falcons area scout**

"The bar has been raised so much in this regard that any legal issues now, especially if pending at the time of the draft or if penalty resulted in jail time, makes you consider taking a guy off the board, or at least sliding him down the pole. There were/are no 'line in the sand' events, but these are NO BRAINERS: any felony charge or domestic abuse now takes guys off (the board) almost 100 percent of the time." – **Randy Mueller, former NFL executive with Seahawks, Saints, Dolphins and Chargers**

CHAPTER 7
The UDFA process

W hen you're a young scout, you have to distinguish yourself to demonstrate you have the stuff to advance. One way you can do that is in the latter rounds and, especially, during the undrafted free agent (UDFA) acquisition process. First, of course, you have to know how the process works and how rookies are processed.

Most of the players in rookie mini-camps are actual rookies (with a few street free agents sprinkled in here and there) in one of three categories: draftees, undrafted free agent signees (UDFAs) and tryout players. Most teams will bring in around 25-30 players between all three categories for their rookie mini-camps.

It's important to understand the difference between these players. Draftees, in most cases, will not have signed contracts. Their agents will take care of that at some point in the coming weeks. Undrafted free agents, in all cases, *do* have contracts. Most sign a standard, no-frills, three-year deal with various signing bonuses (usually ranging between $500 and $15,000). In all cases, tryout players do *not* have contracts. They are competing for the right to sign an undrafted free agent contract. For that reason, tryout players do not count against a team's 90-man roster. It's not uncommon for teams to bring in 20 or more tryout players. What do they have to lose?

I should mention here that tryout players are essentially trying to win a lottery for which the prize is another lottery ticket. A lot of people don't understand that tryout players are seen as the ultimate fringe players by scouts, utter longshots. These days, I see a lot of agents posting on Facebook how their tryout clients are in the league. Well, no, they really aren't.

Because some teams choose to have their rookie mini-camps the second weekend after the draft, tryout invitations are rather fluid. It's not uncommon to see players accept two tryout invitations. Why not? If he makes the team on the first tryout, he can let his agent deal with the other team.

While most UDFA deals are signed in the first hours after the draft, teams may take a week or more before they're done handing out tryout invitations. There's also no set policy on how players get to the team for tryouts. I've heard that some teams will bring in a player for a tryout, but just as often, a team will bring in local players for tryouts so they can contain costs.

The process starts early

One thing to understand is that the UDFA process actually begins weeks before draft day. Teams mostly know who will and won't get drafted, and they begin to focus on those non-draftees early, trying to win them over (sometimes with personalized video messages).

"You start calling the agents a week or two prior to the draft. In our draft meetings, we would rank all of our players in each round. We would also have players that we would give free agent grades. We would have a 'FA – YES,' which was someone we would want to sign if they were undrafted, and a 'FA – NO,' which was someone who was not a reject but someone we would not be that interested in signing as a free agent. We would have someone call the agent for everyone we had ranked in the sixth and seventh round and 'FA – YES' grades. He would express our interest in the player, getting as much information as he could from the agent. He would confirm the phone numbers for the player and the agent and would then tell the agent that if the player does not get drafted, we would be interested in signing him as a free agent. Often the agent would be shocked that we would raise the possibility that his player might not get drafted, and they would tell us how much money they had invested in the player, and that they were sure his player was going in the first three rounds. More often than not, their player would go undrafted. – **Jon Kingdon, former Director of College Scouting for the Raiders**

"Basically, you would start well ahead of time, the whole month of April, trying to get info, talking to kids. At that point, you've identified who's getting drafted, who's in the late draftee/priority free agent range, and the guys not getting drafted. You're reaching out to all of them differently. The late-rounders are realistically possible non-draftees, and you have a pretty good idea of who might get drafted. We did it two ways in New Orleans. Most of the time in New Orleans and Cleveland, it was divided up by position. I was Northeast for the Browns, and I was cross-checking the defensive line last year. It was a situation where, for both Browns and Saints, one scout will have one position, and going in, you'll know how many at that position you want to add. You know you need X players if you don't draft anyone at those positions … Let's say I'm defensive line, so I'm calling guys ahead of the draft in all three groups, and we have them divided into tiers." – **Matt Manocherian, former area scout, Browns and Saints**

Setting it off in the sixth round

Though teams aren't supposed to start negotiating with players until after the draft, that doesn't mean the conversations don't start until after the seventh round ends.

"Once you get to the fifth or sixth round, that's when teams really start calling. You're looking at players that might not get drafted, and trying to get on the horn with those guys and calling them and their agents -- usually the agent first -- and five-ten kids at my position while the draft is still going. You can work your way around that way. One thing you might do is, say you have a third-round grade and you can't figure out why he's not getting drafted and you decide you have to get him. Then you might find the position coach and say, hey, this guy is still available, and if you're both on board, you have the coach call the kid and the scout call the agent. . . Say I'm looking to sign one undrafted free agent quarterback. We're not gonna draft one, and it might be at the beginning of the seventh round, and seven of the 10 on my list have already been drafted. I've called the top 20 (quarterbacks rated as late-rounders) going into the draft, and there are three with draft grades, three priority free agents, and seven more I've contacted. By the sixth round, I've called all that haven't been drafted and then one or two priority free agent guys. If seven have been drafted, I've probably talked to the next eight by the time the seventh round starts. If someone gets drafted and your number dwindles, you might start calling another couple again. I'd say you're in trouble if you're adding guys in the seventh round, but then sometimes you get the guy you never thought you'd have. You assumed he'd go somewhere else, maybe someone you never spoke to, and he ends up signing with you." – **Matt Manocherian, former area scout, Browns and Saints**

"We started calling after the last pick of the sixth round. We would have our position coaches assigned to a scout, and the two of them would have a list and our grades, and we had them ranked by round. Anybody above the sixth round we weren't recruiting heavily because we'd figure they would get drafted. But those with sixth- or seventh-round grades, we thought they might slip, so we might call and recruit them. Prior to (GM John) Idzik, we would recruit going up to the draft, and we would tell a player, 'we'd love to have you, and we don't know what's going to happen draft night.' An area scout would call, and maybe even a position coach would have a list to call so a kid would know the Jets had called twice. We started at the end of the sixth round, and usually once the draft would get going we would let the coaches do more of the recruiting, and the scout would talk to the agent more, unless the scout had a good relationship already, in which case he would be on him, too. Or if the coach knew the agent well, we'd do that, too. . . With (Mike) Tannenbaum, (the scouts) got out of the . . . there was no negotiating. We had a $2,000 straight signing bonus on all the guys. Tannenbaum believed in that but the scouts thought that sucked. When (Idzik) came in, we had different levels based on our grade, and we could go up to $7,000 (that) a scout could offer. If it was someone with a higher than sixth-round grade, we could discuss as a group and go above $7,000 if he was a really highly ranked guy. Most of our guys, we were told, if you can get the deal done between $2,000-$3,000, that saves us money. But everyone does it a different way." – **Jeff Bauer, former Director of College Scouting, Jets**

"There are different ways we've done it, but we mostly call in the sixth round. We meet after the fifth-round pick. In meetings, you start rating free agents, and you make a first, second and third group. So, after the fifth round, you start splitting them up with coaches and call the agents and players and tell them you still may draft them, and you've got groups trying to contact them so they know we're interested, obviously. We start calling at the beginning of the sixth round. We would split up the calls by position, so I might be with the linebackers coach and another scout with the offensive line coach. Usually the scouts call the agent and the coach calls the player. We broke it up into three groups of free agents: one that could be drafted, one that you'll pay a high amount to sign as UFAs, and could be drafted; then a second group is the ones you might pay a little to; and then a third group that might be tryout guys. . . You've got $55,000 for the free agent pool, so you can spend that money any way you want. You could give it all to one player, but it depends on how many you want to get. But if you're paying a guy $10,000 and another guy $5,000, you're still taking the best player. We're not putting an emphasis on a guy making a team based on the money. If he's not good enough, he's not good enough. You're going to give the pick every opportunity to make the team but if he's not good enough he's not good enough. . .

"For me, it was always a cross-check area and position so I would do linebackers and I would be with the linebackers coach and then someone else would cross-check the offensive line and they would be with the offensive line coach. You're working all three groups but you're going with the guys at that position, and you're trying to get the best players available. This is all how (then-GM Jeff Ireland) ran the undrafted free agent signings. I don't remember how they did it in Kansas City with (former Vice

President of Player Personnel Terry) Bradway. When I was with Seattle, you had a group of free agents and you called guys in your area, and that's how you'd work it. (Senior Personnel Executive) Scot McCloughan and (Vice President of Football Operations) Ted Thompson ran the process then, and you were allowed to offer up to $5,000 and if you wanted to go over that, you had to go to Ted. I was on the phone with a kid and (head coach Mike) Holmgren said, 'Come on, Murphy, let's get this thing done.' I had an agent who wouldn't budge, so he said, 'Give me the phone.' And Holmgren said, 'how much is it gonna be to get this kid? $15,000? Done.' Then he said, 'See? This is how it's done,' and I said, 'Give me $15,000 and I'll get it done.' – **Mike Murphy, former area scout, Seahawks, Chiefs, Dolphins and Giants**

Other notes

"At some point, you do need to have bodies to work against. A number of these undrafted players are interchangeable. You might look for a player with big bodies for the OL and DL to work against. You could look for WRs that are not very good but have good speed to work against. Many local players do fit that bill and you can also get some publicity out of the signings. All things being equal, you would rather sign a local player than one who is coming cross country. . . "We would have a fairly large list of potential free agents and we would obviously cross them out if they got drafted. Often times there are players that you gave a fairly decent grade to that would fall to the last round and you would have to get ready to jump on him if he ended up not getting drafted. You would also question yourself as to why a player that you liked had fallen so far." -- **Kingdon**

"Usually the coaches can connect to the kid a little bit better. Probably like twice a year Sean Payton was used as a closer. He would be like, 'Don't bother me,' then 'Oh, that kid? Let me talk to him!' Rob Ryan with the Saints is great. He would trust the scouts, and he would give them a type of guy he wanted, and would trust the scouts to find that player, and Rob Ryan would be very willing to close. He was like, 'Whoever you guys think the best players are, let's go get them and let me know what I can do.' He just wanted the best chess players to play with. You love that as a scout. . . . Coaches are 50-50, unreasonable, only want their guys, and might say, 'I wouldn't take Peyton Manning because I want a guy with arm strength.' And then you have guys like Rob, and most coaches are somewhere in between. (Former Saints defensive coordinator Steve) Spagnola wants a certain kind of player who can do a certain kind of thinking. If you get him a dumb, fast guy, there's not much he can do with that. 'Is this player someone that can play in my system? I don't want just anybody. I want a certain guy.' And Payton knows who he wants, and after that, get him good football players and they will pan out well. One thing that was amazing in New Orleans was how much more often picks were successful on offense than on defense. Definitely that's what makes him great is his ability to figure out what he has and turn it into an offense. He knows what he's looking for, but whatever he has, he's able to adjust. -- **Matt Manocherian, former area scout, Browns and Saints**

"During Idzik's time, he was calling guys, and (Senior Director of Football Administration) Rod Graves would really run the board. With Tannenbaum, it was a contract guy that did it, but with the Jets, (head coach) Rex (Ryan) was like our closer. He would get on the phone and he was the big salesman. It's important to a lot of teams, getting these free agents, getting the ones you want, because there are a couple players out there that can make a team. I think more and more, the last couple years, the scouts took pride in it and the general managers that are personnel guys know how important it is. You can find those diamonds in the rough. . . . Usually offensive tackles are the toughest players to find. If there's one position, offensive tackles can demand more (from their post-draft signing bonuses) than anybody else because everybody needs tackles for camp. But if (the agent for) a receiver is messing around with a signing bonus, (he) better be careful, because there's one just like you out there. I've seen it before. Agents have cost players a spot. If you're an agent, don't try to have three teams on the line because you'll get shut out and have none of them. When you're talking to these new (agents), I would stress over and over, know which teams, based on defensive style and which teams give him the best chance of making it based on position. Those are good agents. Don't quarrel over the money. Know your four or five best teams that give you the best chance of making it. Those agents will have guys make teams. -- **Bauer**

"(Former broadcaster turned Raiders GM Mike) Mayock will talk to scouts. I know he does a lot of tape on his own. He'd come out and try to pick our brains, and he'd talk to personnel directors and GMs, and they got to do their job, and as long as you're not selling the farm, it doesn't really matter. Maybe they talk to Mayock because it's a trade of tidbits. Jeff (Ireland) was trying to not talk to the media, but if you don't talk to them, they will do nothing but stab you. You have to give them a tidbit to keep them happy, and at some point, we told him, you gotta talk to them because they're killing you. . . . What's the hardest position to fill in undrafted free agency? I don't know. Quality ones. Really you can get wide receivers and defensive backs that can run. Finding quality offensive linemen and defensive linemen is tough when you're trying to get quality and not just bodies. You get guys that are bad athletes and they may fall around guys' knees and get them hurt. You want to get better athletes that will challenge your starters, and if you have a bad athlete, you're worried about him hurting your starters, or a wide receiver that can't run. (Former Bears and Packers executive) Mark Hatley used to say, 'we need guys that can run.' They are the ones that can challenge the starters. – **Murphy**

"I've been through the undrafted free agent process with three NFL clubs. I have made it through 16 or 17 drafts, and everyone has been different. All three teams approached them differently. We changed as we went. We grew. We learned. We had really developed a system when I was in Atlanta through a lot of research that basically told us the guys with the highest dip rate in college free agency overall significantly. Sometimes you pay somebody $10,000 or close to that, and they last three days, and coaches decide they don't want them and you move on. That's usually not the case. When coaches work as hard as the scouts do, and you've signed a college free agent to a fairly large amount – which to me is anything over $5,000 -- that's a lot of work that you are investing into that. (The coaches) want them to succeed. Every team has its own unique (UDFA) system. However, it all boils down to this. They all rate players A, B, C, D in terms of levels of free agents. The top free agents are usually guys that everybody thought was going to be drafted, and in that room, they have a draft grade on that player. It could be anywhere from fourth round on down, and if they're still on the board (late in the draft), those players go to the top of the list. Those players who are not drafted go on a college free agent board. They get peeled off that front board, and they go to the top of the (UDFA) list. If you believe in your evaluation system, those are the best players . . . Now, every team's different. I've been in charge, you know, as GM, and twice as college director, so I had the opportunity to run that college free agency (process) at three different locations. We call (UDFAs) unrelentingly, OK? We had everybody call. Why? Because almost everybody in the building is involved in the process. If (an agent) thinks, 'hey, the Chicago Bears really like my guy, he's gotten 10 calls,' well, here's why. You have an area scout that's watching him. You have a positional cross check scout that's watching. In the fall, you have an either national or regional cross-check person, so there's three scouts. There's the college director, that's four. The GM, that's five. Then, the position coach, that's six; the (offensive or defensive) coordinator, that's seven. Then if they like him enough, the head coach is getting on the phone, and that's eight. That's eight people that have touched your prospect on film. They know your prospect, and we want (agents) to know that we know (their clients are) a fit for this team. There's a lot of (scouts) involved in the UDFA process, so (players are) going to get a lot of calls. What I guess I'm telling you is, that's normal. If a club is doing its due diligence, your athlete will get a lot of calls. We called all of them, A, B, C, and D. A's get so many calls, B's so many calls, C's, D's. Even the guys that were D's, which we would call zero dollars-guys (would get calls). There would be no offer, or signing bonus, for them, and it normally would be a tryout player. But even those players got several calls, because those are valuable players. Why? Those players make teams. Undrafted free agency can be crazy. For two-and-a-half hours, boom, you're going at it. Then, if we missed on (signing) everybody (during that two-and-a-half-hour period), we would all go home. Then we'd get up in the morning, and we would

start calling people, checking with agents to see who's still available. And you know what? We'd still have a pretty good chance that two or three of those players could make our roster."
-- Emery

"The coach would start to talk him up a lot . . . leading into the draft . . . like that Thursday, Friday (before draft weekend). He would come down (to talk to the scouts), and say, 'I got a guy.' He would come to the draft room and say, 'I got a guy, (and) wherever he may be on the board, when we need a running back, I got a guy.' One of those situations. The coach, he's putting his neck on the line for that guy in terms of, from his evaluation standpoint, not his true livelihood, but just his evaluation standpoint. So, the coach said, 'hey, I got a guy,' and we went with that. The area scout watched him, and said, 'well, it depends on what you want, but I wouldn't have a problem with that. I wouldn't fight against that.' (It was) one of those situations.

"(Assistant special teams coach Greg McMahon), the position coach who coached Pierre Thomas (at Illinois), had recently been hired to the Saints' staff. He knew what Pierre would bring to the table. So, he knew that every day, Pierre was going to show up, (and) he was going to work as hard as he could. He was going to give his all, everything he could, and he . . . informed us that, you know, Pierre may not be the prettiest, the biggest, the fastest, but he's going to work. At worst, if he makes the roster, he's going to be able to contribute on special teams, because everyone has a role on the NFL team. Whether you're a starter or a backup, you have to contribute on special teams. So, with that said, Pierre came in. Pierre was a need position – an (undrafted free agent) after the draft, and he became that running back who just blossomed into a solid borderline starter and a contributor for the

Saints. He was a guy who showed up every day, did everything, just whatever his deficiencies were, he overcame them. That's the best way to describe Pierre. I can't say anything negative about him. He can't break an 80-yard run; that's his only negative if you think about it. But everything else he does, he does well and you can live with it. -- **Barrett Wiley, former Saints area scout**

"As far as undrafted free agent signings, you have a general framework and a general idea prior to the draft, but you don't necessarily know how a guy will fall. A guy you have as a free agent might be a fourth-round pick, so you don't know until it goes. You typically start to call guys around the fifth round, and if you really want a free agent, you may just draft him late, in the seventh round, so you don't have to compete with the other teams during free agency. What positions are hardest to find? It varies. There's no set answer. It depends on the scheme fit, and depends on the team and how you see players. There's no clear-cut and definitive answer for every single team. It really comes down to how they see a player. You have to also keep in mind that each scout has their own prism and own way of seeing players. Some scouts may have a real hard time finding players, period, because they didn't play or don't have the experience and so forth. So you typically have scouts who are better at finding certain positions than others, but I think it all boils down to the individual at the end of the day. I could find great free agents who were quarterbacks, centers, guards, tackles, but I think every scout has his strengths." – **Aundrae Harris, former Chiefs scout**

CHAPTER 8
Why do players bust?

It's a simple question: what makes a can't-miss player fail?

I asked several active scouts the same question a few years ago, and I got a variety of responses. I expected them all to be a variation of 'you can't measure heart, and you have to really want it, and some players don't,' but it turned out to be much more complicated than that.

Here are few responses that I got back in texts, followed by my comments:

- "GM- and coach-driven draft pick:" I think this response was intended to illustrate that sometimes GMs want a player, but a coach doesn't, and either the player proves to be a bad fit for the team, or the coach doesn't give the player a sufficient chance to succeed. I'll buy that. It's one reason.

- "Reaching for a player because of need. You pass on a great player because you think you are good at that position, (and take) a player not worthy of that slot. You are one injury away from not having a great player at that position:" I think this makes sense, too. Florida State's E.J. Manuel comes to mind. Despite a great series of pre-draft workouts, most scouts I know saw him as a third- or fourth-round pick. The Bills, however, badly needed a passer, and three years later, he's barely hanging onto a roster spot. "It's not the player's fault he was overdrafted," my friend added.

- "There's not a single reason. Each player -- hits and misses -- is unique:" I expected to get this answer from several sources, but most scouts were more specific.

- "The No. 1 thing is they can't play at the mental speed of the pro game. The complexity of the pro game . . . they're not able to handle the mental pressure that is applied by having to play so much faster. It's so much more complicated. You have to watch tape. If guys are slow reactors on the field . . . if QBs hold the ball too long, and don't see progressions, and don't let the ball go, they're never gonna do it in pro ball. If a lineman can't see the blitz, and doesn't pass off well on stunts, there's no way he'll do it in pro football. You get all these wonderful measurables added up, and a coach will say, 'we can fix it.' Most of the time you can't. It's between the ears. It's so much mental. If you can't play strong and sharp and fast, you start to lose confidence, and then you can't function:" I would agree with this, but it's a little hard to measure. How do you predict who will be able to process the speed of the game and who won't? It's not the kind of thing the Wonderlic can measure.

- "Players don't fail! The teams fail for grading a talent that was not good enough based on overrating his talent, or taking him high based on need when he did not belong at that pick, or not smart enough, or the player really did not love football. Those are the players that fail. . . All teams have errors in the first round. There are first-round talents that fail because their addiction, ego or work ethic gets in their way. You can name those. . . Most new GM's were not good scouts. Their decisions and record tell the tale:"

There's a lot to unpack here. On one hand, it's true that some players just don't want it, and others who are put in situations where they can't win. Then again, the new model for GM hires is still a bit unproven. As coaches get more power in the scouting process, it's logical that there will be misses.

- "I'd say a quarter or maybe even a third of the time the player is not coached/developed like scouts think he should be. Happens all the time. Majority of the time, if you take a guy high, the player will at the very least have the traits -- height, weight, speed, athleticism, etc. -- so it's extremely hard for a scout when you feel he's not getting developed properly. And maybe a third of the time you missed on the guy's talent. He just wasn't good enough, good as you thought he was. Another third, you miss on the person. You didn't realize how the kid was wired, whether it's toughness, motivation, mental capacity, whatever reasons:" These are fairly common reasons that others have named, though it's interesting to see the splits.

- "Definitely, it is more often than not getting a bad match with a system or coaching staff. Oh, maybe would say 50/50. I have seen coaches and been told, 'man, who do you want to make it? We totally control who plays and who looks good.' Actually, (our defensive coordinator) told me that sitting with a couple of scouts one night. I saw it with (our head coach) and his staff. If you brought someone in they did not like, he had no chance. (That's) totally why personnel and coaching has to be on the same page, because a lot of (coaches) do not like personnel guys telling them, 'this guy is good,' when what they saw they thought (at the Senior Bowl, or during limited film study), he stunk, wanting to prove they were right. (Our head coach was) totally like that. Oh, (our head coach was) nice and fun to scouts until there is a difference of opinion on a guy and he does not get the guy he wanted. But there are some (head coaches) who know that none of us are right 100 percent of the time, but they respect the process:" This is a great point. Coaches have tremendous power at cuts time, and I've heard that many are not above tilting the board to make some players shine and others falter.

I think draft success is a function of talent and ability, mixed with system and ability for a team to adapt to a player's talents (and vice versa), and finally, where a player is drafted. First-rounders get paid reasonably well, but for many players, a switch flips and the hunger isn't the same as it is for a fourth-rounder who thought he was going at the top of the second round.

There are probably many more theories on why players don't make it. Here are a few comments from scouts on why some players make it and some don't.

"Let me explain something to you there, too. Would you have ever heard of (NFL great) Brett Favre if it hadn't been for (former Packers head coach) Mike Holmgren? Would you have ever heard of (NFL great) Joe Montana, if it hadn't been for (former 49ers head coach) Bill Walsh? You can go on and on like that, and sometimes it's just the luck of the draw and you get with the right team, the right system that knows how to utilize you. I believe Wes (Welker) went to San Diego first, and nothing came out of that (**Editor's note**: He went to camp with the Chargers, then spent two seasons with the Dolphins), but you can go on and on with players like that, and the league and just happened to be the marriage at the right time, and you can probably put (former Cowboys quarterback) Tony Romo in that category. Would it have been Tony Romo coming to the Cowboys without (former Cowboys QBs coach) Sean Payton being there? – **Jim Hess, former Cowboys area scout**

"Now, I really don't like using the term 'being right' on players because most of the time there are so many circumstances (player work ethic, injuries, opportunity, system, scheme, coaching, mental makeup of the player, character, talent of the roster and yes, even a little luck) around each athlete that factor into a player's chances of NFL success. You better be 'right' more often than not. . . To really know if a player has lived up to his draft status, he will need to perform at a particular expectation level for an extended period of time. We drafted a second-rounder who did start and was a solid contributor for three seasons before an injury shortened his career. I guess you can say we were 'right' in that situation. Make no mistake about it: you (even personnel types who have tons of experience) will be 'wrong' on players , but your 'hit ratio' is much better if you can draw on your football experiences." – **Ken Moll, former Browns and Jaguars area scout**

"(Saints running back Mark) Ingram came down after a Thursday night game this year. Ingram bucks the system. When he first came into the league, he tried to do it his own way. It wasn't until he got humbled that he decided to do it right. I went to Flint (, Mich., Ingram's hometown) to meet him personally before the combine, and he chose somewhere else (Sonic Boom in New Orleans). He performed awful. (Wisconsin OG) John Moffitt had a better broad jump and shuttle run! Ingram ran a 4.6 (40), his vertical was bad, it was awful. He still didn't come here after his first year, but then after his second year in the NFL, that's when he came and he started listening, and became a believer. He bought a Shredmill (a treadmill-like device that Villani patented), and then he bought a house down here, and I think it's shown. That's how (former 49ers wide receiver) Anquan Boldin and (Bucs OB) Lavonte David and the Pounceys (Dolphins OC Mike and Steelers OC Maurkice) and (Redskins wide receiver) Pierre Garcon all do it. They build their offseason around their offseason training. Not where their girl is, not anything else. They can party, do what they want, but they gotta build it around their offseason." – **Tony Villani, owner of Boca Raton, Fla.-based XPE Sports, one of the top combine prep facilities in the game**

"(The) stage can be too big at times. Coming from small schools, crowds are small. The NFL has bigger crowds and more negative voices. The ability to make plays in the crunch can (also) be a factor. Too much free time, no classes to attend. The player has to learn time management and being a pro, (avoiding) outside influences or hangers-on, as we call them. Example: taking care of your homeboys or other friends and not staying focused on your job as an NFL player. Baby mama drama is a factor, also." – **Bruce Plummer, former Falcons area scout**

CHAPTER 9
War Stories

When people find out I work in the football business, they always want to hear stories about the business. Hey, I'm the same way. Who doesn't love a great story? With that in mind, I've dedicated this chapter to several random stories about the business that I've heard over the years. Some are interesting, some are funny, some are surprising.

I'll get things started with a story of my own from the first year of the College Gridiron Showcase, an all-star event that I'm proud to be a part of. This takes place in the first year of the CGS, 2015, in Arlington, Texas.

Tuesday was weigh-ins, maybe the most important event of the week for the 106 players on CGS rosters. For National Football Scouting, which always conducts weigh-ins, it's always a hassle getting the players where they're supposed to be, then getting them lined up and into their shorts so they can be weighed, measured and paraded across the stage so team officials can check out body types.

As everyone assembled that Tuesday, there were three players still unaccounted for. This is quite routine. After several phone calls and rooms checked, game organizers found two of them, but a third was still MIA. Turns out there was a good reason for that: he was being stalked by his "baby mama."

The story we heard was that this young man was behind on child support. He had been tracked down by the mother of his child, who lived in the Dallas area or nearby. Intent on getting her money, she started blowing up his phone early in the morning, challenging him to produce the necessary funds or risk her showing up and causing a big scene in front of scouts and team officials.

Apparently, the gamble worked, and he was ready to make good, but there was a problem: she wasn't waiting around for weigh-ins to conclude. That meant that, in the middle of weigh-ins, the young man had to find an ATM. Fast. Only, he couldn't find one in the hotel lobby, so he had to run across the street to a convenience store, half-dressed, where the frustrated former paramour was waiting. He quickly withdrew the money and sent her on her way, keeping scouts waiting to get his height and weight.

The story has a happy ending for all concerned. After sprinting back across the street, he stripped down to his shorts, stepped on the scale and satisfied the needs of the assembled evaluators.

Falling down (and getting back up) in Florida

Here's another good story that, while not about a scout, I heard while on the all-star trail (so I think it counts).

In the 1990s, before the internet, ATM cards and Venmo, handling finances was a lot different. When coaches were going out to recruit, schools handed them a wad of traveler's checks -- I'm not even sure if these things still exist -- and sent them on their way.

At this time, there was a particular coach who was not especially disciplined. In fact, during his time as an assistant coach in the early '90s, his team had been reluctant to send him on the road, fearful he might get himself into trouble. Eventually, the team relented, sending him to South Florida, around Miami. What could happen, right?

Plenty happened. In his first days in South Florida, he discovered jai alai, which was exceptionally popular in the area in the late '80s and early '90s, especially with gamblers. Back then, pari-mutuel wagering and jai alai went together like Miami and vice. In the space of a day or two, two things happened. One, the coach got a crash course in jai alai. Two, he became dead broke.

That left him with few options. There were no cellphones, and what would he say if he called the school anyway? For the coach, a burly sort, there was one thing to do: find the bars on the Hispanic side of town, where he had an idea.

He'd wait for things to get busy, then challenge a fellow bar patron to arm wrestle. Arm wrestling was this coach's game, and this became his hustle. For several nights, he spent the evenings arm wrestling for $10 a match, then sleeping in his car.

At this point, fortune smiled on him. Details are scarce, but either he was able to locate a former coach in South Florida, or he bumped into a friend one night at the bar. Either way, he found a sympathetic ear, and his friend allowed him to sleep on his floor. Now the coach had access to a phone and non-vehicular lodging.

From there, with a small loan from his friend and his earnings toppling arm wrestling enthusiasts, the coach went on a whirlwind recruiting trip, hitting all his stops and making all his contacts before returning to the school. It all worked out, though odds were against it almost from the start.

Party pooper

Seattle has acquired a reputation for being very thorough not just in its scouting but in evaluating players that will go outside the top 100 players, and obviously, it's paid great dividends.

With that in mind, the Seahawks took an all-hands-on-deck approach to interviewing players, with head coach Pete Carroll himself getting out and speaking to selected players. One of them was Rob Blanchflower, a tight end from Massachusetts who, despite a great career at UMass, had missed the Senior Bowl with a leg injury. This created a bit more mystery surrounding the pass-catcher, as teams weren't able to do the normal level of due diligence.

Within that context, Carroll stopped by for a quick chat during the interview phase at the combine.

"Rob, nice to meet you and talk to you," Carroll said. "You seem like a really good guy. Tell me a little about yourself. Have you ever been in trouble? Done any drugs?"

"I drink a little," Blanchflower replied.

Eager to make sure "a little" didn't mean two cases and a bottle of scotch per day, Carroll followed up with another question.

"What's that mean?," he asked.

"I drink when we celebrate," the tight end said.

Starting to get a bit concerned, and probably thinking he might have tripped up on an area of concern, Carroll asked for clarification.

"What does that mean?" he asked again.

At that point, the Minuteman sensed a brewing storm he needed to head off, and he knew exactly how to do it.

"Coach, we were 1-11 last season," Blanchflower said.

Positive reinforcement

In 1981, John Paul Young had just arrived in New Orleans as part of Bum Phillips' staff with the Saints. Bum, John Paul and the new staff had been brought in to try to capture the energy and excitement Phillips had created in Houston as part of the 'Luv Ya Blue' crew that challenged the Steelers for AFC supremacy in the 1970s.

The Saints made a bold move in the 1981 draft, passing up North Carolina's Lawrence Taylor for South Carolina's George Rogers with the No. 1 overall pick. As the narrative has developed, in that draft, this was just another Saints blunder in an early team history chock full of them. What people don't realize is that the Saints could take their 'new Earl Campbell' with the top pick because they hoped another elite linebacker would be available in the second round. That player was Rickey Jackson, whom they took with the 51st pick.

From there, as the Saints' linebackers coach, it was Young's job to groom Jackson and get him ready to be an impact player. However, things got off to a bumpy start.

As a new member of the team and someone learning a new defense, Jackson was not yet instinctive in his first couple practices. During film sessions, Young consistently corrected him, in a teaching manner but firmly and directly. This seemed to embarrass Jackson, who was clearly down in the dumps after one such session. Eager not to lose his star pupil, Young took him aside to encourage him.

"What's the matter, Rickey?" he asked a visibly pouting Jackson.

"Nothing, coach," the 'backer replied.

"Come on, Rickey, what's the matter?" Young prodded.

"You're always on me, coach," Jackson responded.

Concerned that Jackson would be so easily hurt, Young expressed concern.

"Well, Rickey, when you were at Pittsburgh playing for Coach (Jackie) Sherrill, didn't they have to fuss at you sometimes?"

"Nope, coach, never."

"Really, Rickey? Well, what would they say to you?"

"All they ever said to me was, 'Attaboy, Rickey!'"

Here are a few more good anecdotes from around the game.

"In 2001, I was the positional cross-check guy for wide-outs for the Chicago Bears. It was my first go-round with the Bears during that time, and I'll tell you a little story. (Wisconsin WO Chris Chambers) will always be in my memory bank because I was pushing for (him) hard. I mean, I loved those big hands, and that catch radius, and all that end zone work. (He) had a catch where (he) went up over the top of a corner of an end zone and grabbed a one-hander. And it was so beautiful. It was such a moment of grace and athleticism, and just beautiful to see, and that's the reason I'm in it, OK? Because I see this as art. This brings joy to my heart to watch somebody do something that no other human being can do. It's special, and that catch was special. So, we're having a little debate about (him). And so, I was the positional cross-check scout, I had wide-outs, and I stack all the wide-outs in the country from one on down, OK? This was way before digital (film), OK? This is VHS and 16 millimeter tape. We were responsible for making the profile and cut. So what I did is, I stuck it on that catch, and repeated (his) catch 10 consecutive times so that everybody got the feel about how I felt about (him). So, Mark Hatley, our Vice President of Player Personnel at that time, said, 'Hey Phil, that's enough.' -- **Falcons national scout Phil Emery, who has also scouted for the Bears and Chiefs and served as Chicago's GM from 2012-14**

"I had to cut Alonzo Spellman in the AFL. Scariest damn day of my life. I almost thought about just keeping his ass when he walked in. I don't know if you've ever seen Spellman in person, but I mean, holy s___, he's the biggest human being. He's got a 6-pack at 315, and he didn't look like he'd slept in 10 days. I almost s__ my pants when he walked in the room. I literally thought about not cutting him as a coach. I was like, maybe we don't have to cut this dude. I'm looking around like, I might not get out of this room. I don't ever feel that way about a player, but that's a scary dude. And I mean, I'm being funny, but I don't blame him. I'm being funny, but the guy's got mental problems, it's sad, it's really sad. -- **Danton Barto, former area scout, Rams**

"(Saints WR) **Marques Colston** was almost cut due to speed. I mean, (Coach Sean) Payton said, what am I going to do with this guy? He can't run. He showed up out of shape at mini-camp, but when he came back later in the summer, he was in better shape, and not running as badly, and they started to figure out a role for him pretty fast. And by then he had a great rapport with Drew (Brees). Lance Moore and Colston would never have played in the NFL if not for Payton. He just knows how to use a player." – **Matt Manocherian, former area scout, Browns and Saints**

"Dominic Rhodes was at Midwestern State (in Texas). Back then, I was a national cross-check scout (for the Falcons), and I was in the Dallas area . . . covering another school, and I thought I'd run into the school. Another guy had gone and seen him and given him a free agent grade. He was about 5-foot-8 and a half, 5-9, a short guy, and about 205 pounds, but I saw him run real fast, and I like speed, you know, and athletic ability, and I saw he had some stats, and he could really (play). I went and looked at film and tape on him, and then I stayed over on Saturday and went to the game. Shoot, the game I was at, I think he was at 200-some yards rushing, and did all kinds of stuff, so I wrote him up to be like a third- or fourth-round pick and make somebody's team. The other (scout), I know what he was looking at was the fact that this was a Division II school, he doesn't play against the great big guys . . . but when you're a skilled athlete, a receiver, a defensive back, a running back, I don't care who you're playing with. If you can do it, you can do it. He just stood out so much. What ended up happening was, I was at Atlanta at the time and Dan Reeves was our coach, and . . . I wrote him up good. This other guy had just given him a free-agent grade, and for some reason or other, our Director of Player Personnel at the time put him as a free agent. We didn't talk about him in our meetings, so Dan didn't know anything about him. Well, he gets drafted late by the Indianapolis Colts (Rhodes was actually signed as an undrafted free agent after the '01 draft), and doesn't play, like, the first 5-6 games, and then they come and play at Atlanta, and the starting running back (**Edgerrin James)** gets hurt. Dominic starts the game and gets like 170-some yards rushing (Rhodes ran for 177 yards on 29 carries with two TDs in a 41-27 Colts win). I get a telephone call Monday from Dan, and he said, . . . 'this guy runs so well.' I said, 'just go look at my grade,' which he did." -- **Bill Groman,** former Oilers and Falcons scout

"I am trying to think of specific players but there was an argument in Dallas where there were two (defensive backs) on the board, and I wanted one over the other, but was overruled by the head coach. We got both of them, but I was mad that it happened the way it did. The player I wanted stuck, where the other was released. Now, it has happened the other way around, as well, (where I) felt good about getting a player but (he) currently has not panned out like I thought he would or should. The worst one that stuck with me was (OT) **Cordy Glenn** from Georgia (who went on to be drafted in the second round by the Bills in 2012). I had some people on my side (with the Dolphins), but when it came down to the last meetings before the draft, the whole room had changed. Something happened, and now there was a consensus that Cordy was overweight and had weight issues, which I vehemently disagreed with. We took (OT **Jonathan) Martin** from Stanford, but Buffalo took Cordy the pick before, so it was a moot point, but (I was) very discouraged with the flip in the room and some of the comments made about the player which were absolutely false." -- **Mike Murphy, former area scout, Seahawks, Chiefs, Dolphins & Giants**

"We boiled down after meetings, and evaluations, and going to the combine and working out in the spring and this, that, and the other thing, it kind of came down to either (NC State DE) Mario Williams or (USC running back) Reggie Bush. What was really fascinating was that we had one big meeting where most of us were in there with (Texans owner Bob) McNair and some of his people from the business side, and they had two coaches. Bob Karmelowicz was the defensive line coach for the Texans at the time. He loved Mario Williams. Chick Harris was the running backs coach. Harris was a proponent of Reggie Bush. So, they did this presentation in front of Mr. McNair and Chick did a good job, but he kind of let the film do the work. You know, you put up Reggie Bush on the film and let it go. He was a Heisman Trophy winner, and he was fast and quick and really had a productive season. (Harris) kind of let (the film) do the work. Well, Karmelowicz was this type of guy . . . he was just a real character. Just an unbelievable character. He was one of these guys that when he got on somebody, boy, you'd have thought he was the best player ever. So, he put on the film, and he would stop it, and he'd say, 'now, the angle of his foot is in a position that he's going to plant and drive, and he's got this acceleration,' and all this. He just went overboard in the explanation of what he liked about Mario Williams. I think it sold a lot of people that this was the better selection.

"So (GM) Charley (Casserly) had a big meeting in the scouting room, and everybody was in there, all the college scouts, all the coaches that were on the staff, and the pro (scouting) staff. I think it was the week of the draft, because we hadn't made up our mind yet. I think Charley had made up his mind, because Charley had kind of liked Mario Williams in the preseason. He liked him all the way through, but he wanted everybody's opinion. So, everybody went around the room, and they had their opportunity to say what they thought the strengths and weaknesses of the different picks would be. One of the more interesting picks was the offensive coordinator, who at the time was Troy Calhoun,

who is now the head coach at the Air Force Academy. He had been with the Denver Broncos for a while, and he made a great point -- and I was kind of surprised because I thought all the offensive people would want the running back, Reggie Bush, and the defensive people would want Mario Williams. But Calhoun came up and said, 'you know, with our offense we've always had success in the running back position regardless of where we took them in the draft. (In Denver), we didn't take high draft picks, and their running backs were still successful because of the system that they ran. They ran this zone concept of blocking and everything, so they took running backs in the fifth and sixth round, and they became all-pro.' So, he brought that point up, and I thought that was a really interesting point, that he thought that they could pass on a running back. They didn't need him in the first round, and we could take the defensive lineman and get a running back down the road. So that's what we eventually did."
– **Miller McCalmon, former Bills and Oilers assistant coach and former Redskins, Lions and Texans scout**

"We were in meetings, and it was early, if I can recall, maybe about 4 or 5 (p.m.) . . . and some (news) started trickling down, and whispering. All of a sudden, they told us, I'll be back, we've got to go, and then (head coach Sean Payton and GM Mickey Loomis) were gone for about an hour, and we're sitting there twiddling our thumbs, with nothing to do. So, they come back and told us, 'y'all can take off. Be back tomorrow.' Now we knew that something's not right. . . That was unusual, because we weren't getting out of those meetings until 10, 11 o'clock around there, late. So, me and another scout jumped in the car, and we're going to grab something to eat. All of a sudden my phone starts ringing. It was from a guy that used to work with us a year before. He's like, 'hey man, I heard y'all getting Reggie (Bush)?' I was like, 'Whoa, where'd you get this from? You're with another team.' So right then and there, we kind of looked, and we're like, that's what that deal was about! That's what that deal was about. That had hit way before the media had got it out, and we figured, now we knew. We didn't know we were getting him, but we kind of knew that that's what we were kicked out for now. That's why we were asked to come back tomorrow. It was a need-to-know basis, and we didn't need to know. They felt that that's their prerogative. They didn't want anything leaked. But I mean, goodness gracious, a guy from another team had already called about it. And so, the next morning, when we came in, of course, that night it was all over that Mario had worked out an agreement (with the Texans), and that Reggie was (available). And that next day we went in, and that was a no-brainer at that point. If Reggie had gone to the Texans, Mario was not (our pick). If I can recall, probably, I think it may have been (Ohio State LB) A.J. Hawk. I guess that's OK to say now. . . We watched the tape, and he's running around, he's active, he's doing what he does . . . So, I think everybody saw that, and if I can recall . . . if we had to go Saturday morning and take the paper up to the podium, I think it was A.J." -- **James Jefferson, former Seahawks safety and Saints area scout**

"When I was with the Chiefs, height, weight and speed minimums were an important thing. Everyone who works for (former Chiefs scouting executive) Bill Kuharich, and for (Alabama head coach Nick) Saban too, everyone has HWS parameters by position, but that never really overrides if the player is good. If you want your cornerbacks 5-10, but he's (5-9 1/2) but great, it doesn't stop you from drafting them. The thing that takes precedence is if the player is good. Can he help you win? Typically, those things take precedence. Really, at the end of the day, it comes down to how your GM sees it. There are some GMs that wouldn't take a 5-7 cornerback – for instance, (former Chiefs GM) **John Dorsey** would never take a 5-7 corner. It all just depends on what your philosophy is for a given position." – **Aundrae Harris, former Chiefs area scout**

"If it hadn't had been for (Bears Vice President of Player Personnel) Mark Hatley, (the Bears wouldn't have taken Brian Urlacher). Nobody else wanted him. I had to get up on the table for them to draft him. Of course, now they all say they wanted him (chuckles), but they didn't at the time, I tell you that. In fact, several (members of the personnel staff) were highly pissed at me until he got to camp. He was playing strong safety (in college) and (New Mexico) would bring him down in the box anytime it was a run situation, which made him like a 'monster' back (a free-lancer who moves to the strong side of the offensive formation), and even when he was in the secondary he was making plays at the line of scrimmage. On a lot of plays, (New Mexico) wasted his ability. He should have been in a position at free safety because he had a better opportunity to get to more plays. Anyway, as you watched him, you would probably draft him in the middle of the draft as a defensive back. But after I watched him, I got fascinated by him. I met him the first time I was there, and . . . we just connected. I probably spent a lot more time looking at him than anybody else did, and I just felt like he had a lot of the same characteristics that I looked for in linebackers. You can't put it on paper what it is. It's just a feeling that you get from watching hours and hours and games and games of film."

"The big question was whether to go offense or defense, and we needed to draft a quarterback sometime, during that draft. Just like most clubs, offense is a lot dearer to them than defense, so there's always that. If you're going to draft a defensive player in the first round, there's going to be some opposition. You've got those guys that are 'take the best athlete available' guys, they're height/weight/speed, and then you have those guys that are position-oriented, and it's good if you have a spread to cover all those areas. Myself, I'm a guy that looks for a player that can make a difference, a player you can build something around, whether it's a running back or a tight end or a quarterback or a free safety or a linebacker. Remember, (former Chiefs linebacker) Dino Hackett out of Appalachian State, that was a similar (draft) situation, and there was a lot of opposition between second and third round (Hackett was drafted 35th overall). And you know, (Saints linebacker) Rickey Jackson was another one. But Urlacher, he just was a guy that the Good Lord blessed him with the ability to get to the football and diagnose plays, and that showed up when he was playing free safety. After we drafted (Urlacher), the coaches, when he came to camp, put him at Will linebacker, which is like safety, a hybrid safety position. Mark Hatley called me and said, 'You'd better get up here,' so I went up there and we had a knockdown, drag-out fight, this time with the coaches. Me and Mark had to get film out and show them, and anyway, they said they'd try him there for a little while. He made Rookie of the Year and Pro Bowl the first year in the league. I've made plenty of bad choices, and had plenty that didn't work out, just like anybody, but this is a team sport, and a guy's got to fit in to the team. (He) has to bring something to the team and has to enhance the team around him. You don't hire a quarterback to win the ballgame. You hire him to help the other 21 win the ballgame. I don't have all the answers, but (I believe that)." – **John Paul Young, former NFL assistant**

coach with the Oilers, Saints and Chiefs and former scout with the Bears

"I don't think (former NFL WR Wes Welker) went to the combine, but I was at his pro day, and he didn't look very good. He didn't run very fast, and he's not very big. . . I didn't really think I could sell him to Coach (Bill) Parcells, and I really didn't try. I put a free agent grade on him . . . and in my write-up, I said, 'this guy could be a steal in the fifth, sixth or seventh round.' Why? Well, he had produced. Totally produced everywhere he had been. Player of the Year in Oklahoma. All-American, or at least all-conference, at Texas Tech. Punt returner, kick returner, great hands and great quickness, but I knew Bill wouldn't draft a guy like that. Not that small. And you have to admit, Welker, you didn't hear of him in the pros until he got with the Patriots." – **Jim Hess, former Cowboys area scout**

"We didn't need a wide receiver at that time, but we got down to the seventh round, and (Marques Colston) was pretty much the shining star on the board. You have a guy with all the measureables, the physical attributes that you want in a receiver, a project wide receiver, and we couldn't risk trying to take him as an undrafted free agent, so that's why he was drafted in the seventh round (252 overall). I wanna say he like ran a 4.53-4.55. He wasn't a blazer, but let's clear up a misconception.

"To the average person, to anyone who's not a professional athlete, if you naturally run a 4.55, or if you naturally run under a 4.6, you're fast. If I can pull you out of bed, let you warm up, and you can run a 4.55, 4.57, 4.51, you're a fast human being. If you're a guy say that can run a 4.31, 4.22, whatever the outlandish times are, those are the guys who are rare. That's Olympic. They can trade a football for an Olympic baton, and if, someone who's 6-4 ½, 6-5, and 204-205, that's moving pretty fast. Randy Moss, he may run a 4.3 or 4.4, but that's a freak of nature. Whenever you hear guys who are running the 4.4s, those are the guys that are freaks of nature. As a combine scout, in the spring, I would time 300 guys. Out of that 300, I would get maybe 25 guys who would run under a 4.6. That tells you right there the percentage of the natural population because, in the springtime, I was evaluating those guys before they went to the speed camps, the personal trainers, all they had was the trainers at their schools. Now, at the bigger schools, the guys would be more advanced physically, but at the smaller schools like Marques Colston's (Hofstra), or Jackson State, or Arkansas State, a school that had . . . the program might not be year-round or maybe not as in-depth as a bigger program. If a guy runs a 4.51, I know in the spring when I come back after his senior season, he'll be a 4.45, maybe a little bit faster once his technique becomes better and he has specific training for this particular drill.

"And then going back to the part about the overall natural speed, you see a guy who runs a 4.5 or lower, might have been five out of 100 in the grand scheme of things. That's why the misconception about getting caught up in speed, the number on his card at the combine or his pro day doesn't necessarily mean what he plays to. You can have a guy who runs a 4.6, and if I'm not mistaken, (49ers great) **Jerry Rice** might have run a 4.65, something like that, but he was never caught from behind and outran cornerbacks. You know, his game speed and his time speed sometimes are two different things. A guy like Colston, he's a big guy, and you might think he's slow and lumbering but he has the ability to get up on cornerbacks quickly and get open and catch the ball." – **Barrett Wiley, former Saints area scout**

"I'll never forget the day I was visiting a particular school, and after watching tape all that morning, a particular offensive lineman really caught my eye. The only question I really had, and with good reason, was his intelligence. I kept seeing what I saw were countless mental errors, but his physical ability was hard to overlook. Finally, I caught the offensive line coach before practice and asked him, 'just how smart is the kid?' His reply left me no closer to the answer than when I walked through the door that morning. After a long pause, the coach gave me his most honest and very well-thought-out answer: 'His intelligence is somewhere between a moron and a genius.' Another time, the player I studied that day was a great athlete in major D-IA program. In fact, he was special enough to start at receiver on the football team and point guard on the basketball team. I was visiting the school in late November and asked the head coach if the kid was going to play basketball after the football season. The coach rolled his eyes, smiled, and replied, 'Why don't you just go ask the kid?' After receiving permission, I did just that. The player's reply was classic: 'I don't know, coach. There's a slight chance of maybe.'" – **Bears executive scout Jeff Shiver, the first winner of the C.O. Brocato Memorial Award for Lifetime Service to Scouting in 2020**

ACKNOWLEDGEMENTS

It's a tired expression to say "this wouldn't be possible without the help of so many people," but the truth is that this book wouldn't be possible without the help of a lot of people.

First, I want to thank my editor, Paul McGrath, who's not only an excellent rotisserie baseball commish but also a tried-and-true eye when it comes to cleaning up my mistakes and giving me feedback on my writing style.

I also want to thank my friend, Bruce Plummer, who's quoted in this book and who's become a good friend over the last few months. He's already proven he's a good scout to so many, and he richly deserves to be back in the NFL. I also want to thank his daughter, Madison, who's getting ready to head to Starkville to begin her own career in sports. She took the photo of her father that I enhanced a bit before putting it on the cover. In Madison, Mississippi State is getting a good one.

I also want to thank my sons, Jake and Zach, who are both on their own respective athletic paths. Their hard work, dedication and intensity inspire me, and their love and respect fulfill me.

Obviously, my parents, Walt and Paula Stratton, have been a critical part of my journey, too. That's why I'm excited to dedicate this book to them.

I also want to thank my girl, Polly. I dedicated my first book to her, but nothing I've ever done professionally would be possible without such a faithful companion. She is truly a blessing from God.

Speaking of God, last but not least, I want to thank my Lord and Savior, Jesus Christ, for the hope and love and truth that comes from knowing Him.

Made in the USA
Middletown, DE
09 September 2020